Controversy and Psychology

Controversy and Psychology examines a range of areas studied in psychology that have sparked controversy, encouraging readers to think critically about the research they engage with in order to develop their own opinions by recognising biases in this discipline.

Author Phil Banyard investigates the popular, mainstream subject of psychology through a critical eye, presenting a researched account of how the discipline, practice, research methods, and theories of psychology have focused on a narrow group of people and in so doing brought harm to others. The controversies addressed in the text include methods in psychology, the history and ongoing acceptance of racism in psychology, the categorisation and quantification of people, the excessive and unhelpful use of diagnostic categories, the involvement of psychologists in warfare, and finally the role of psychologists in persuasive messaging. This illuminating text explores the history of these controversies and highlights how they continue to affect the profession and its interactions with people.

Controversy and Psychology is an essential read for undergraduate and pre-undergraduate students studying psychology and for anyone in related fields looking to gain a broader knowledge of the more contentious aspects of the discipline and enhance their critical thinking skills. Professionals and researchers looking to re-examine their working methods can also benefit from the book.

Phil Banyard has recently retired from the Department of Psychology at Nottingham Trent University, though remains affiliated with them as an Emeritus Professor. He was a Chief Examiner of A Level Psychology for many years and has written more than 20 texts.

Controversy and Psychology

Philip Banyard

LONDON AND NEW YORK

Cover image: © Getty Images

First published 2022
by Routledge
4 Park Square, Milton Park, Abingdon, Oxon OX14 4RN

and by Routledge
605 Third Avenue, New York, NY 10158

Routledge is an imprint of the Taylor & Francis Group, an informa business

British Library Cataloguing-in-Publication Data
A catalogue record for this book is available from the British Library

Library of Congress Cataloguing-in-Publication Data
A catalog record has been requested for this book

ISBN: 978-0-367-70698-2 (hbk)
ISBN: 978-0-367-69899-7 (pbk)
ISBN: 978-1-003-14758-9 (ebk)

DOI: 10.4324/9781003147589

Typeset in Bembo
by MPS Limited, Dehradun

Contents

Figures

Tables

Preface

If you are looking for a measured and 'balanced' account of some discussion topics in psychology, then this is not the book for you. For a start, I don't believe that balance is achievable because to have balance you have to decide on the balance point, and that already places you within the argument and not apart from it. This is my account of how psychology has been part of activities that brought harm to people.

The first edition of this text was written 20 years ago and I have found it interesting to reflect on how my ideas and understandings have changed in that time and also how my writing style has changed. I think the first edition was much more jokey and looked to sugar some bitter pills. I seem to have lost my sweet tooth.

When you write something that highlights problems in the behaviour of others it is very easy to be self-righteous. I hope the text does not come over in this way. The problem for psychology is not so much that a few people do bad things but that the rest of us don't speak up about it and therefore tolerate these actions being done. We are complicit in these actions by not opposing them.

Acknowledgements

In the first edition of this book 20 years ago, I acknowledged the contribution of my parents in encouraging me to have my own opinions and giving me the confidence to express them. I would like to endorse that sentiment now.

I would also like to acknowledge my students who have over the years challenged me to be more critical of my ideas and assumptions and my colleagues who have indulged my rants. For this book, I'd like to thank Deanne Bell who has guided me to a better (though still limited) understanding of the racism that exists throughout our society and damages the lives of so many people on a daily basis.

No work is even done alone and I have been supported by so many. A special mention to Amelia and Christian, Cece and Evaline, Nicky Hayes, Cara Flannagan, Jean Underwood, Kitty Fisher and all those people who have intentionally or inadvertently helped me to reflect on my ideas and the world that I live in.

Phil Banyard
Nottingham

1 Why is psychology controversial?

This book was originally titled, Controversies *in* Psychology, but that didn't fit. This book concerns controversies *about* psychology. There are lots of issues in psychology that promote debate such as the nature, nurture debate or the question of whether psychology can be called a science. This book is not about these issues though some of them crop up as part of other arguments. This book is about the controversies that have been generated by the activity and ideas of psychologists. It is about the controversy of psychology itself and what it stands for. The following chapters develop issues around psychological methods, racism in psychology, the many attempts to quantify human experience and the role of psychologists in war. In this chapter, we look at some general issues that underpin psychology and also at the aims of psychology and how it is taught.

Psychology's place in the world

The point of psychology

Psychology provides a window onto human experience and behaviour. Indeed, Abraham Maslow was moved to write,

> I believe that the world will either be saved by the psychologists or it won't be saved at all.
>
> (Maslow, 1958, p. 27)

And he has a point. The major issues that confront us in the early years of the 21st century are mainly created by ourselves or require behavioural solutions to fix them. Climate change, racism, starvation in some parts of the world, obesity in others, global pandemics, war – the list is massive. All these crises require changes in the behaviour of people to improve the situation. And that's where psychology comes in. The problem is, however, that psychology has not always been on the side of the angels and that is what this book is all about.

Psychology gives us some clues about who we are and what we can become. It can contribute to our understanding of what we can do and achieve

DOI: 10.4324/9781003147589-1

as individuals, and also help us to create a society that we are comfortable to live in and proud to be part of. In my view, and I grant you this is a partial one, that society will give equality of opportunity to all people, distribute wealth fairly, and will be outward looking (taking an international perspective rather than nationalistic one). Of course, all these things are much easier to say than to achieve.

Agent of social change

You might see psychology as a scientific subject that uncovers knowledge and therefore does not have a role as an agent of social change. My answer to this is that I see psychology as a moral science of action (Shotter, 1975) rather than a natural science. It studies behaviour and provides insight into how we can bring about individual and social change. It is inevitably an agent of social change, so the issue is to establish what principles of change it is supporting, and who are the beneficiaries of that change.

In answer to the point about science, I would argue that all science has a responsibility to the society it works within and maybe also to humanity (one small step for man …). Over the last half-century, psychology has positioned itself as a science. One of the reasons for this is the credibility that science has but also for the additional funding that science courses in universities have attracted. Part of the belief in science in the Western world is that it has a moral code in its own right and doing things 'for science' is justification enough.

The problem with the moral invisibility that the cloak of science gives psychology is that it is based on a false metaphor. In the commonly held view, science is discovering truths and rolling back the clouds of ignorance. For example, we might observe that astrophysicists are uncovering information about how the universe works at the macro- and micro-levels. It is hard to argue, however, that psychologists are following this same pattern and un-covering new information that allows us to stand on the shoulders of giants and build up the knowledge of our science. Research in psychology is not so much about uncovering knowledge as inventing it (see chapter 4 on diagnosis for examples of this).

Maintaining the status quo

Psychology is a well-funded mainstream subject in the United Kingdom and the United States with the amount of research funding from government agencies alone measured in hundreds of millions of pounds in the United Kingdom (Wakeling, 2010) and billions in the United States (APA, 2017). On top of that, there are over 75,000 undergraduates studying psychology each year in the United Kingdom (OfS, 2021) generating income to universities of over £700 million per year from fees alone. Psychology is big business! And as such, it has an interest in maintaining the status quo and keeping the business going.

Maintaining the status quo is not a neutral position. In a society where the major institutions support the privilege of the few at the expense of the many, maintaining the status quo puts you clearly on one side of the divide. Elsewhere in the book, we look at the impact of psychology on racism over the last hundred years, and its role in supporting powerful professional elites. This is not to say that all psychologists are actively promoting the status quo because they are not. There are many critical voices but as an enterprise, psychology is not challenging the institutions and the oppressive practices even though it has clear evidence to do so. Sometimes, it is not just what we do that is important but also what we tolerate other people doing unchallenged. This issue is discussed further in chapter 3 when we look at racism.

Think about the qualifications we offer our students. At my institution (Nottingham Trent University), we aim to value and celebrate the achievement of our students (as do all other universities). The majority of psychology graduates at undergraduate and postgraduate levels are female. We celebrate their achievement by giving them the title of Bachelor or Master, and if they do well in an academic career they might become a Fellow. The irony of continuing to confer male titles on women at the same time as offering courses in gender studies is difficult to take. You might think that these titles are a trivial example and it's just words that come from a long academic tradition. Language is important, however, and our daily discourse has many terms that reinforce a status quo that is misogynist and racist (and that's just for starters). The example above is easy to fix but such is the commitment of universities and their psychology departments to the status quo that it does not even appear on the agenda.

Controversies *in* psychology and controversies *about* psychology

What are controversies? I guess there is a controversy whenever there is more than one point of view. So, for example, I think that SpongeBob SquarePants is a fantastic cultural creation but not everyone agrees and some people see it as a gay propaganda (BBC, 2005). We have a disagreement and some might call it a controversy.[1] If we take this approach into psychology then we will find that everything is controversial because for every piece of evidence that is put forward, there are a number of interpretations of that evidence. Psychology, and all other sciences, develop through debate and controversy. It is a part of how they operate. In the context of this book, however, the term controversy has a special meaning.

Some arguments and debates have an extra edge, perhaps because of the consequences of the debate or because they challenge people's core beliefs. In

---

1 But like many things that we call a controversy they are manufactured and trivial and are given airplay just in order to generate clicks on websites.

psychology, there are some issues that can have a very serious effect on our daily lives and so have been the centre of fierce debate. For example, labelling people as intelligent or unintelligent can have life-long consequences (see chapter 5 for further discussion of this). Psychology also looks at why people behave in the way they do and makes some suggestions about what is human nature. This inevitably challenges some people's moral, political and religious beliefs. It is these debates that we will look at in this text. The underlying themes of these controversies centre around the control and manipulation of people, the perceived differences between one group of people and another, and our beliefs about human nature.

Control

Who controls whom? If psychology achieves its ambitions and is able to de-scribe and affect the behaviour of people then who should be allowed to control whom? Say, for example, we find a way of changing people's attitudes and behaviour very effectively, should we use this to stop young people from starting to smoke cigarettes? This would have a long-term benefit because it would improve their health and reduce the amount of money they spend on drug consumption. This all sounds like a good idea, but what about if we then use the same technique to encourage people to think badly of marginalized and socially ostracised groups?

The behaviourist J.B. Watson suggested that the aim of psychology was to develop a technology that can control people. For example, in his 1924 book *Behaviourism* (reprinted in 1930) he wrote,

> The interest of the behaviorist in man's doings is more than the interest of the spectator – he wants to control man's reactions as physical scientists want to control and manipulate other natural phenomena. It is the business of behavioristic psychology to be able to predict and to control human activity.
>
> (Watson, 1930, p. 11)

The ability to be able to predict and control my own behaviour is very useful. I will be able to choose how to act rather than to react unthinkingly to changes in my environment. The ability to predict and control someone else's beha-viour, on the other hand, raises a number of ethical and moral issues. So, it is important to know how psychological information will be used and who will use it on whom. Watson was clear on who should have the information,

> If psychology would follow the plan I suggest, the educator, the physician, the jurist and the businessman could utilise our data in a practical way as soon as we are able, experimentally to obtain them.
>
> (Watson, 1913, cited in Shotter 1975, p. 32)

This view was endorsed by B.F. Skinner in his book *Beyond Freedom and Dignity* (1972). In this, he argued that we need to develop a technology of behavioural control to improve conditions in our societies. For example, he wrote,

> The real issue is the effectiveness of techniques of control. We shall not solve the problems of alcoholism and juvenile delinquency by increasing the sense of responsibility. It is the environment which is 'responsible' for the objectionable behaviour, and it is the environment, not some attribute in the individual which must be changed.
>
> (Skinner, 1972, pp. 76–77)

Skinner believed that our behaviour is moulded by our environment rather than motivated by our personal values and beliefs. According to Skinner, the reason I behave well or badly is not because I am a good or bad person but because of the reinforcements and punishments I have experienced in my life. Therefore, my bad behaviour is not my fault and I can stand up in court and say 'society is to blame, your Honour'. If you follow this argument through then you end up with Skinner's suggestion that we need more control in our society and not less. And that control should be used to give people the re-inforcements and punishments that encourage good behaviour (whatever that is).

The ethical question for psychology is whether it should be used by governments to control people and create an ordered society, or whether it should be used to enhance personal freedoms. There is no obvious answer to this and the question has to be struggled with by each new generation of scientists.

Giving psychology away

A different point of view to the above was put forward by George Miller (1969) in his Presidential Address to the American Psychological Association. Miller pointed out that according to its constitution the object of the American Psychological Association is to promote human welfare. But what does this mean? Whose welfare is being promoted, and at whose expense? He said,

> Understanding and prediction are better goals for psychology and for the promotion of human welfare because they lead us to think, not in terms of coercion by a powerful elite, but in terms of the diagnosis of problems and the development of programmes that can enrich the lives of every citizen. (p. 1064)

> Our responsibility is less to assume the role of experts and try to apply psychology ourselves than to give it away to the people who really need it. (p. 1064)

Miller suggested a very different aim for psychology from that suggested by
Watson and Skinner. I guess it is for the reader to decide which side they have
greater sympathy for, though for my part, I would endorse the general sentiments of Miller, and I have a lot of concerns about any attempts to use
psychology to control and manipulate the general population, even when it
may appear to be 'for their own good'.

The issue of control runs through most of the following chapters and the
information presented largely challenges the contribution of psychology. To
add some balance, however, psychology has also been used to achieve a lot of
positive changes, but not surprisingly, these changes are not so controversial,
and so do not get much coverage in this text. I wouldn't want the reader to get
the impression that the bulk of psychology is an exercise in exploitation
conducted by an army of amoral scientists. This text, however, aims to look at
the controversies in the subject and so concentrates on the more disturbing
aspects of psychological research.

Individual and group differences

Psychology makes a lot of statements about differences between individuals
and differences between groups. Comparing individuals to group norms and
comparing groups can have some positive applications, but there is real jeo-
pardy in going down this route. If we want to make statements about the
differences between people, we need to be able to take reliable and valid
measurements of psychological variables. We also need to have a clear theoretical understanding of what we are measuring (these issues are discussed in
chapter 4 on quantifying people). If we want to go further and make statements about differences between groups of people, then we need to be able to
define the groups of people and have measurements that can be applied to all
people (these issues are discussed in chapters 2, 3 and 4).

If we are making statements about differences between individuals and
between groups we have to be mindful of the social and political consequences
of this work. For example, if an individual or group of people are defined as
being inferior to other people, and it is suggested that this inferiority has a
genetic component,, then one response to this will be to discourage these
people from having children. In case this sounds extreme, be aware that
Psychology has a long history of promoting (by the few) and tolerating (by the
many) eugenicist arguments that have been used against the poor.

Human nature

What is human nature? The model we have of human beings affects our
judgements of their behaviour and their intentions. What does it mean to be
human and what parts of my behaviour are inevitable? Misogyny is a common
and pervasive feature of our society. Is it part of male nature to behave like this
or is it something that can be challenged and changed? You can see that the

answer you choose will have an effect on how you think things such as sexual harassment and domestic violence should be dealt with.

The question is sometimes framed in terms of which characteristics of human behaviour are due to genetic programming and which characteristics are due to our social environment. Behaviour that is largely under genetic control cannot be adjusted through social interventions such as education, whereas behaviours that are largely under social control are open to greater adjustment. This simplification, however, masks a much more complicated state of affairs, and therefore a much more complex argument. It is obviously part of our nature to breathe, and also to eat. Without these two behaviours, we die very quickly. However, the act of eating, though a biological requirement for survival, is also under a lot of social control. The way that we eat, the things we choose to eat, where we choose to eat it and who we choose to eat with, are all aspects of eating that vary from person to person, and culture to culture. So, it is in our nature to eat but the way we eat is modified by social influences.

The reason that this debate generates so much heat is because the view of human nature we choose will lead us to certain solutions to the perceived problems of society. If, for example, we believe that violent and criminal behaviour is due to genetic features of the individual we might try and deal with it by surgical attacks on the brains of violent criminals or through the sterilisation of offenders. The practical and ethical problems with this solution means that it is not at the front of modern debate, but it is a logical development from these arguments and, as we will see in chapter 4, these policies have been enacted.

So where does this leave us in our debate about human nature? My suggestion (and I hasten to add that I do not claim this to be original) would be that human language gives us a good model for examining human behaviour. It would appear that there are a number of biological features that structure human language, for example, there are specific brain sites for key features of language comprehension and production. There also appear to be a number of universal features of all languages, and this suggests some form of genetic structure to the way we develop this skill. However, there are hundreds of different languages in the world, and we are able to use language in an infinite number of ways, for a wide range of purposes. I would argue that our biology provides us with a range of abilities and opportunities, but the way we develop them and choose to use them is affected by our social development and our personal interpretation of the world.

Summary

Psychology is a moral science of action that provides insights into human behaviour and experience. There are issues about who has control of that knowledge and what uses they put it to. The default is to create a powerful elite who control the knowledge, but there are alternatives to this approach.

The teaching of psychology

Before we get on to the major controversies of psychology in the following chapters it is worth looking at the teaching of psychology. It is one of the most popular subjects at A Level and undergraduate level and we are creating a society that is psychologically literate. A back of an envelope calculation suggests that over one million students have studied psychology at school in the last ten years alone in the United Kingdom. This is perhaps psychology's greatest contribution to our society – bringing the ideas and curricula of be-havioural science to the masses. In this section, we are not going to look at the curriculum of these courses but the way they are taught.

Study and play

In his Presidential Address to the BPS, Tony Gale (1990) challenged us to apply psychology to the teaching of psychology. He painted a negative picture of the way psychologists deal with their own knowledge. In a delightful rant, he argues that

> ... we produce passive learners, respecters of authority, and students whose primary purpose in learning is negative reinforcement and the removal of anxiety ...
>
> (Gale, 1990, p. 483)

Gale also looks at the concept of power and argues that the role of the teacher is to liberate the learner's mind and to shift some of the balance of power from the teacher to the learner. The problem is that we have created all-powerful assessments where the most strategic way of achieving success is to adopt a passive role and learn and reproduce the set answers. The economics of education mean that class sizes are large in schools and colleges, and massive in universities. The dynamics of large classes are that the teacher inevitably adopts a more powerful role – 'I have the knowledge, you will listen and take notes.' And the dynamics of assessment mean that the examinations become the purpose of the course rather than a necessary addition. The students therefore see themselves as taking the course in order to get an A Level or to get a degree. The absurdity of this becomes even more pronounced when we consider the nature of these assessments later in this section.

Gale's solution to some of these issues is to radically change the focus of laboratory classes. Commonly, these are seen as the opportunity to drill learners in the techniques of research and the precise way to write up research reports. An alternative view would be to try and recreate the primary school class in the laboratory.

> My way of learning how to be a psychologist is to provide students with a playroom and appropriate resources. Every student should be able to

sample, at their leisure, the principal approaches to measurement and their application within substantive areas. (p. 486)

This approach focuses on the intrinsic pleasure of finding things out by doing them and of illuminating the wonder of psychology for our students.

Play is a complex concept to define and in part, it is a matter of self-definition (Wood & Attfield, 2003), but for our purposes here let's see it as a contrast to work. If we see work as serious, purposeful, useful and worthy, then play is fun, and not necessarily purposeful, useful or worthy. And yet it is clear that children develop cognitive and emotional skills through play and probably rather more than they do through work (Wood & Attfield, 2003). The value of play can be seen in the digital technologies that have been introduced into schools in the last 20 years. Children describe how they enjoy using these technologies and describe some of the learning activities as play (Hall & Higgs, 2005). If we follow Gale's idea, we will turn all laboratory sessions into playtime. Despite the MacDonaldisation of our education system (Ritzer, 1993), there is still room to allow our students to personalise their study of the personal science and to dive into the blooming, buzzing confusion of psychological knowledge.

Assessment

Assessment is seen as a key aspect of education courses. Ranking students is what we do, and psychology, as we will see in chapter 4, is very adept at quantifying and categorising people. It is not clear why we choose to assess academic progress by ranking students, and it is one of the puzzles of modern life that there is so little challenge to this process especially given the lack of evidence to support it. We just take it as given that we need to give students grades and degree classifications and ensure that any award they have has a male name.

The assessments which are largely conducted in the United Kingdom use traditional (i.e., pre-digital technologies) techniques, and focus on traditional (i.e., pre-digital technologies) academic skills. The origin of these techniques in UK education can be traced back through the University of Cambridge Local Examinations Syndicate (UCLES) to 1858 when a group of academics were invited by some Durham schools to develop assessment techniques for their pupils. The lessons were observed in order to capture how the pupils were being taught. Tests were devised to match the teaching and learning that was taking place. The techniques for external examination are largely the same today even though the style of teaching and learning has moved on dramatically. There is a clear need to create assessments that better measure the shifts in learning activities that accompany the effective use of digital technology. For example what form of assessment best captures the move from essay to storyboarding or the rise in visual as opposed to verbal presentational skill.

The examination essay is seen as the untouchable gold standard of assessment. When I was at university in the 1970s, this assessment mirrored how I might create a written piece. I would do the research, prepare the notes and then write the essay as a single and final piece. At coursework and at examination, the process was similar. Today, I would never construct a piece like that. I draft and edit, draft and edit. And current students will never have experience of this traditional process except when they are being assessed in examination. For their coursework, they are required to create their work digitally using the technology of the computer and the writing style of draft and edit. This in part mirrors their learning. In their examinations, however, they are assessed using the technology of the Biro using a writing style that is unique to the assessment process. What validity can we claim for this process? The assessment does not match the learning and does not even relate to anything that they will be required to do when they leave school or university. It is indefensible but constantly defended.

In addition to the validity issue about the examination, there is a reliability issue. The reliability of essay marking has been seriously questioned for a long time (e.g., Jones, 1938, Newstead & Dennis, 1994). One solution to the reliability issue has been to introduce double marking and this has been found to be increase reliability (Brooks, 2004) but the dramatic increase in UK psychology undergraduates during the last decade has made this process impracticable in many universities. So, in summary, we are basing the key assessment of an individual on a measure with poor reliability and questionable validity.

The solution is to stop defending the indefensible and instead struggle with the difficult task of devising assessments that are valid measures of the learning we require our students to do.

The difficulty in addressing assessment is that it performs two major functions. First, it provides an indication to the student of their progress and allows them to reflect on their work and adjust their learning. Second, performance on assessments is used to examine the perceived effectiveness of teaching at the level of the individual teacher and also at the institutional level. This second point makes it strategic for teachers to provide assessments that are easy to administer and easy to teach to. This approach makes it strategic to 'teach to the test' (Halonen et al., 2003) and in so doing minimise the more sophisticated and subtle aspects of student learning.

The strategic approach to assessment influences the student learning (Conner-Greene, 2000) and as it becomes strategic for the student to focus on the text we end up with a spiral into meaningless assessments where …

> … students may not engage in more advanced kinds of study skills because the course exams and other assignments simply do not demand it. … Teachers may verbalize the need for students to develop more sophisticated study strategies but do not provide the demands and practice that would promote this development.
>
> (Bol & Strage, 1996, p. 159)

Summary

Psychology is a major player in education in schools and colleges. It provides courses that conform to the current pattern of education in the United Kingdom which uses pre-digital techniques and tasks to examine students many of whom have only known digital technologies (digital natives?). It is a further example of psychology contributing to the maintenance of the status quo which, as we will see in chapter 3, has inbuilt biases that provide hurdles for people from historically marginalised groups.

In this text, I try to present a number of controversial issues in a way that allows the reader to develop their own opinion on them. I do not, however, pretend to be without bias, and I have strong opinions about most of the issues covered in the next six chapters. You will not need to be a rocket scientist to spot my biases, though you might like to consider whether other psychologists also have biases and whether you can spot them in their writings.

2 Psychology's methods: Are they all they are cracked up to be?

Psychology asks great questions about the widest range of topics. They include detailed and highly technical questions about brain function, and deep thinking questions about what it means to be conscious. The subject deals with all you want to know about life, the universe and everything. The key unifying factor that stretches across the range of psychology's interest is its focus on evidence. To obtain this evidence, psychology has developed a wide range of methods and techniques of analysis. The focus of this chapter is to look at whether these methods and techniques actually deliver on the claims that are made for them. We will look in turn at the following controversies:

- The myth of objectivity (can psychology be objective and is objectivity even a good thing?)
- The replication crisis (is psychology broken?)
- Do Psychology's methods discover anything of value?

The myth of objectivity

The focus of Western science has been to create evidence that is objective and can challenge the irrational beliefs and superstitions to which we are all prone. Psychology is largely still influenced by this empiricist tradition, which holds that knowledge comes from the senses (what we observe), and that evidence should be gathered using the scientific method. Psychology aims to provide statements and theories based on evidence rather than opinions and revelations. The issue here is whether psychology is indeed detached and free from opinions and bias and whether this objectivity is achievable or even desirable.

To be objective is usually taken to mean standing apart from the subject that is being studied, and being free from bias. This might be possible if we are studying objects such as rocks or micro-organisms, but is it possible to be objective when we are studying the people rather than objects? It is difficult, if not impossible to stand apart from the subject when that subject is human behaviour and experience and you are a human being. And if we try to be objective about people we risk starting to deal with them as if they are objects. In this section, we look at some of the problems psychology has with the

DOI: 10.4324/9781003147589-2

attempt to be objective and we will come back to the issue of the bias in psychology throughout the text.

Balance

Scientists pretend to be objective, that is free from bias and free from value, but can this be achieved? You can't help but view the world from a particular perspective, that of yourself and the various groups to which you belong. I cannot be free from bias because my behaviour and conversation are affected by the way I interpret the world and the opinions that frame these inter-pretations. Examples of these biases are racism and sexism and we look at these elsewhere in the book.

Sometimes psychologists attempt to take a balanced view. The problem with this is that it presumes that we all agree where the middle of two op-posing arguments, and hence the balance, should lie. To take an extreme example, imagine taking a balanced approach to child sexual abuse. Should we position ourselves mid-way between someone who opposes adult–child sexual contact and someone who advocates it? This a clearly a non-sense. So we have to accept that the choice of the balancing point is not a matter of detached objectivity, but a matter of opinion.

Balance and objectivity do not appear to be possible. What is achievable, however, is to be aware of your perspective and the limitations it imposes on your view. Psychology, unfortunately, is often blind to its perspectives and biases. In the next section, we will go on to look at three sources of bias in psychology that come from the way it carries out its investigations; average people, the differences between and within groups, and invisible people.

Average people

Many psychological studies are designed to look for measures of differences between groups of people or between conditions. These studies rarely look at individual diversity as one of the key features. It is more common for the participants to be treated as identical people and for the 'participant variables' (psychology speak for our individuality) to be kept to a minimum or ignored. This reduces people to biological widgets. This means that the conclusions of the research can only produce statements about how 'most people' or the 'average person' will behave. But who is this average person, and what do they think, feel and do? And, is it reasonable to assume that most people are 'average'?

Engineering Psychologists (ergonomists) measure the dimensions of dif-ferent parts of the body to see what is the best possible design for machinery. Designing a car seat is a good example. The seat needs to be comfortable for most people that would want to drive the car. The obvious strategy would be to design the seat for the '50th percentile person' – the person who is average on all, or almost all, of the body dimensions. The dimensions include standing

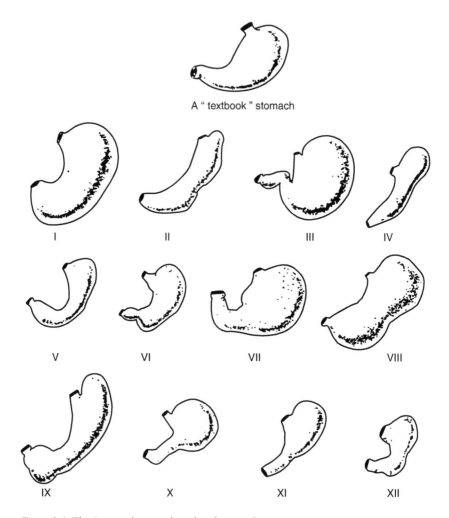

A " textbook " stomach

I   II   III   IV

V   VI   VII   VIII

IX   X   XI   XII

Figure 2.1 The 'average' stomach and real stomachs.

height, sitting height, arm reach, knee height, shoulder breadth, etc. It is unlikely that any one person would be exactly average on a whole battery of dimensions, but we could reasonably expect a number of people to be in the middle third of most dimensions. Unfortunately, this is not so. A study by Daniels (1952, cited in Gregory and Burroughs 1989, p. 65) investigated the body dimensions of 4,000 flying personnel on just ten dimensions. They found that not one person fell in the middle third for all measurements. Nobody had an average body, or to put it another way, there was no average person.

Another example of this individual diversity can be seen in the diagrams of stomachs shown above (Figure 2.1). A comparison of the drawings of 12 'real' stomachs with a textbook drawing of a 'normal stomach' shows that none of the stomachs are 'normal' and many do not even look like stomachs.

If there is no such thing as an average body, it seems rather unlikely that there is such a thing as an average personality or an average behaviour pattern. When we talk about averages we mean that we have added up all the scores and divided by the number of measurements taken. This average score does not have to describe the behaviour or personality of even one person. So, when psychology texts and research papers talk about how people behave, they are referring to a theoretical average person, and it might well be that no real person actually behaves like this.

Differences between groups and within groups

Another problem that comes from looking at average scores is that you can come to some inappropriate conclusions about group differences. For example, there is a lot of interest in the differences in performance between men and women. If you take the average score of men on some dimension and compare it with the average score of women you might find a small difference. However, the spread of scores within males and females far outweighs the difference between the two groups, and of course, not everyone fits into these two categories. Also, with regard to gender differences in children, for example, reviews of the research into cognitive ability and social behaviour have consistently found that there are very few measurable differences, and in the cases where there is a difference the effect is very small (for example, Woolley, 1910, cited in Williams, 1987; Maccoby and Jacklin, 1974; APA, 2014; Jäncke, 2018).

Look at the example distributions below (Figure 2.2), they show the different distributions of boys and girls on a made up variable of 'binkiness'. You will see that girls have an average binkiness score a little higher than boys, but that the

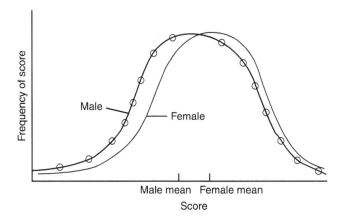

Figure 2.2 Distributions of 'binkiness' in boys and girls.

distributions overlap so much that it would be impossible to predict a person's binkiness score just by knowing their gender or vice versa. An analysis of the research on the development of social and cognitive behaviour found that male–female differences accounted for only 1%–5% of the variance in the population (Deaux, 1984). This means that gender is a very poor predictor of how an individual will behave. This example illustrates how we can obscure individual experiences and behaviour by losing them in meaningless average scores.

Invisible people

A further problem with the idea of the 'average person' is that some groups of people are excluded. Any minority group is, by definition, going to have only a small effect on the average. These groups of people are therefore excluded from the discussions about behaviour and experience. The 'average person' is white, heterosexual, a parent, waged, able-bodied, binary, and so on. This 'average person' becomes the default in discussions about behaviour and experience and obscures the lives of people not fitting this pattern.

Our concepts of average or normal behaviour contain a number of assumptions and biases. A study by Broverman et al. (1971) into what doctors expect of healthy people illustrates this problem. In this survey, doctors were asked to identify the terms that best described (a) a healthy adult, (b) a healthy man or (c) a healthy woman. There was good agreement between the doctors on what were the characteristics of each group. The characteristics of the healthy man were judged to be very similar to the characteristics of a healthy adult, which is what we would expect. The characteristics of a healthy woman, however, were significantly different from the characteristics of a healthy adult. One of the inferences we can draw from this is that when doctors think of an 'adult', they are assuming that it is male. Although the term appears neutral, it carries some hidden assumptions and biases.

So, there are adults and there are also women. If we take this a step further I would suggest that there are also the following assumptions in our language:

- There are people and there are Black people.
- There are people and there are LGBT+ people.
- There are people and there are people with disabilities.

I could go on, but I don't want to labour the point. We need to be aware, then, that apparently neutral terms such as 'people' actually contain a lot of assumptions.

When we use the term 'people', we do not mean 'all people' but just 'average people'. What this means is that a large number of people are invisible in psychology texts. In fact, we do not even notice that they are absent. This may not matter if the experiences of these people were the same as the experiences of the 'average person', but they are not. We will explore this further in chapter 3.

The controversy that hangs over psychology is that much of its research is presented as being objective. This objectivity is seen as being independent and detached from political or moral positions. This might be possible for material sciences but, as I have argued earlier, this is not a credible position for studies of people. We always have a position and an opinion, and our work is about people and not objects, and by purporting to be objective and detached psychologists are in danger of missing the core of what it means to be human.

The replication crisis (Is Psychology broken?)

We have some reasonable expectations of science. We expect that it is rigorous, the results are replicable and the report has been reviewed and endorsed by other scientists. Let's briefly look at these terms before exploring whether psychology lives up to this.

Rigour: Scientific rigour is the strict application of the scientific method to ensure unbiased and well-controlled experimental design, methodology, analysis, interpretation and reporting of results.

Replicability: Replicability is the ability to repeat the study and get similar outcomes.

Peer review: Peer review is the scrutiny that scientific papers go through before publication where the work is reviewed by scientists with no connection to the work.

Since the first psychology laboratory was established 150 years ago, the subject has blossomed into a massive worldwide enterprise with thousands of departments and laboratories. Psychologists publish well over 100,000 scientific articles every year in over 2,000 scientific journals. Some of these articles gain traction in the popular press, some have an effect on psychological practice and some appear in texts for students. The world is awash with psychological information but how reliable is it? How confident can we be about the psychology we read?

Things are not always what they seem

Psychology textbooks and many courses in psychology use key historical studies to illustrate psychological ideas. If you have studied psychology then you will probably have come across eye-catching studies such as the Milgram Obedience Study, the Stanford Prison Experiment, the Hawthorne Effect, Rosenhan's Sane in Insane Places and many more. They are grand studies with powerful findings and they are great to study (and fun to teach).

Unfortunately, many of these studies do not conform to the rigour that we expect of science. A recent review of the data that Milgram collected found a different story to one he presented (Haslam & Reicher, 2017), and there are questions about the data in the Rosenhan study (Cahalan, 2019). The picture of psychology from these classic studies (of which the above are just two examples of many) is that they provide moral stories that help us reflect on our own behaviour and the behaviour of others, but they are not scientific studies that have rigour, that are replicable or have been subjected to serious peer review.

Looking at it like this, you can see psychology as a secular replacement or addition to religion. It uses stories of moral acts to provoke discussion and guide us to a better understanding of our behaviour, and hopefully to learn about to behave with greater humanity. It is difficult, however, to see these studies within the framework of science.

Although these studies are very prominent in psychology courses they do not reflect the majority of studies published today which are subject to peer review and conform more closely to our expectations of science. But, there are serious issues that have been raised in the past ten years about the conduct of psychological research.

Recent frauds

Some cases of outright fraud brought a sharper scrutiny on what psychology is doing. One of these involved Deiderik Stapel who was professor of Social Psychology at the University of Groningen in the Netherlands. He published articles which often caught the public imagination, for example, an article published in the prestigious journal *Science* which purported to show that messy streets with litter and broken bicycles promote stereotyping and dis-crimination. The report contained data from two field experiments and three laboratory experiments.

The studies, however, were never carried out and Stapel had merely created the data himself. Following reports from three whistleblowers, Stapel was investigated by his university and admitted to systematically creating the data. Over 50 scientific papers were then retracted, but this is not the end of the issue and further examples of psychologists creating their own data came to light. The problem is how all this work was accepted by journals and how the peer review process did not manage to spot the problems. This casts a cloud over the whole peer-review process and hence the rigour of the psychology we read in the journals.

The concern about scientific journals is not limited to Psychology. After receiving a spam email from the *International Journal of Advanced Computer Technology*, Peter Vamplew sent an anti-spam article as a reply to the spam email without any other message, expecting that they might open it and read it, but not that it would be considered for publication. However, the journal accepted it as a paper and sent him an acceptance letter and comments from a reviewer. The 'article' was entitled 'Get me off your f****** mailing list' (without the asterisks) and was entirely made up of those seven words repeated over and over again (see Scholarlyoa). The acceptance of nonsense, or in this case abuse, is by no means an unusual event for academic journals. In 2005, three graduate students in the United States created a programme that gen-erated scientific-sounding nonsense and used this to get a (nonsense) article accepted for publication. The programme is free to download (SCIgen, if you are interested) though it is not clear how many people have used it to create bogus paper. However, in 2014, two major publishers withdrew more than 120 papers that had made it into their journals even though they were computer-generated gibberish (Nature Communications, 2014). Among the titles were gems such as 'Application and Research of Smalltalk Harnessing Based on Game-Theoretic Symmetries' and 'Simulating Flip-Flop Gates Using Peer-to-Peer Methodologies'.

The above examples are in no way unique and merely illustrate a serious problem with the scientific process. This is not saying that it is completely broken, and it is important to say that there are no serious concerns about the majority of published work. But it is clear that the review process is not as robust or reliable as we expect.

p-Hacking

One of the most widely used criteria for accepting an experimental effect has occurred is the *p*-value. A *p*-value is a measure of the probability that an observed difference could have occurred just by chance. The lower the *p*-value, the lower the probability that these results could have occurred by chance and the greater the statistical significance of the observed difference. The accepted value for statistical significance in most psychology journals is $p < 0.05$ (sometimes referred to as the 5% level).

If your study has statistically significant results it is more likely to get published. And if it is more likely to get published then the researcher is more likely to get rewards such as grants and promotions. Generally speaking, for a scientist to progress in their career, or to even have any career to begin with, they must publish regularly. You can see a possible conflict of interest here between scientific rigour and career development.

This brings us to *p*-hacking which can be defined as the manipulation, whether intentional or not, of statistical testing procedures in order to obtain a desired outcome. One way to achieve this is to throw all the statistical tests you can find at your data and select out the results that get a *p* value < 0.05 while ignoring the rest. You then partially report your analyses focusing on the significant results. It's not dishonest but you are putting the most positive spin you can on your work. This then leads to what is termed the file drawer effect whereby academics end up filing away all their non-significant findings in their proverbial desk drawer. This has major ramifications for the field because important findings are then never shared.

The miracle of the 0.05 significance level

And then, there is the miracle of the *p* values. If you remember from above, the generally accepted level for significance is a probability of 0.050. This means that if your analysis shows a probability of 0.050 or less then everyone is happy and the result is deemed to be significant. Your study has supported your prediction and publication (and promotion) are more likely. If the analysis shows a probability of 0.051, then everyone is sad, your prediction is not supported, you don't bother to submit your article for publication and you start looking for another job.

Don't despair, however, because a miracle seems to occur when your results are close to that critical level. Masicampo and Lalande (2012) found an exciting phenomenon. When they looked at the p values reported over a year in four major psychology journals (which amounted to 3,627 p values), they found that there were far fewer at the 0.051 level (just not significant) than you would expect. The chart in Figure 2.3 illustrates their results.

Somehow or other, the studies that were near to edge seemed to have just made it over the line. Perhaps they had been nudged or perhaps this is one of the effects of p-hacking, it is not possible to tell. But this illustrates another aspect of the research process that demands our caution when reading scientific papers.

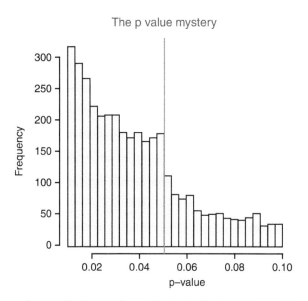

Source: Masicampo EJ, and Lalande DR (2012). A peculiar prevalence of p values just below .05. *Quarterly journal of experimental psychology* PMID: 22853650

Figure 2.3 The *p*-value mystery.

Replication studies

To try and address some of the issues described above, psychologists have started to carry out some major replication trials. In a report published in 2015, the Open Science Collaboration describe an attempt by 270 psychologists to replicate findings from 100 studies published in 2008 in prestigious journals (Open Science Collaboration, 2015). The Reproducibility Project is designed to estimate the 'reproducibility' of psychological findings.

The headline result from the Reproducibility Project report is that only 36% of the replication attempts showed a statistically significant effect. Or to put it another way, two-thirds of all studies could not be replicated to get the same result as the original. Some replications found the opposite effect to the one they were trying to recreate. This is despite the fact that the Project went to incredible lengths to make the replication attempts true to the original studies, including consulting with the original authors.

This doesn't mean that the original studies were faked but it does question how quickly we should accept a result before subjecting the study to replication trials and further scrutiny. The positive spin on this is that although these results are disappointing it does show Psychology as a trailblazer for examining its practices and trying to introduce more rigour, or am I clutching at straws?

Research re-examined

The growing concern about scientific rigour has led to many established findings being revisited, including,

Social priming: Social priming is a general phenomenon whereby subtle, possibly unconsciously perceived, stimuli prime attitudes and behaviours. A classic example of this (Bargh, Chen, & Burrows, 1996) was a study in which words that were related to elderliness, such as old, lonely, grey, primed participants to walk more slowly than controls when leaving the study. This study in particular and many related studies could not be replicated in numerous independent attempts to do so (see Doyen et al., 2012).

Facial feedback: The facial feedback phenomenon generally described how one's facial expression affects one's mood or emotions. In particular, it has been claimed in a famous study by Fritz Strack (Strack, Martin, & Stepper, 1988) that participants who were forced to smile by holding a pen in their teeth found cartoons funnier than when they held the pen in their lips, which forced them to pout. In a recent multiple independent lab replication attempt (Wagenmakers et al., 2016), involving thousands of participants, this effect could not be replicated.

Imitation in babies: It has been claimed for over 40 years that newborn infants have an innate ability to imitate facial expressions (see Meltzoff & Moore, 1977). A recent study (Oostenbroek et al., 2016), involving 106 infants tested on multiple occasions between their first and their ninth week after birth, found no evidence that newborn infants can reliably imitate either facial expressions or actions or sounds.

Ig Noble Prize: Something fishy here

One last thing to look at this section is illustrated by an excellent study by Craig Bennett and his colleagues who published a paper titled 'Neural

Correlates of Interspecies Perspective Taking in the Post-Mortem Atlantic Salmon: An Argument for Proper Multiple Comparisons Correction' Bennett, et al., 2010), for which they won an Ig Nobel Prize in Neuroscience. The Ig Nobels are like the Nobel prizes only better. They are awarded for science that first makes you laugh and then makes you think.

The researchers were preparing for a study with human participants in which they planned to scan their brains during an experimental task. They wanted to test the experimental set-up and scanning equipment and in order to do so, they enlisted the help of a large Atlantic salmon. The salmon was given the task instructions, put in the fMRI scanner, and completed the experiment. Afterwards, the experimenters analysed the data and noticed that an area of the salmon's brain showed significantly different readings between the experimental conditions (with $p < 0.001$). This is remarkable in itself, but even more remarkable when you find out that the salmon was dead.

If we discount the possibility that the fMRI scanner brought the salmon back to life, then we can see that it is possible to get rogue readings from this very complex apparatus. It shows a further problem with accepting p-values as the main judgement of significance.

Summary

The above sounds like a tale of complete woe that paints psychological, and indeed all scientific research in a very poor light. My take on it is that there is such pressure on psychologists to publish and hence to obtain significant results that sometimes rules are bent a little, but for the most part, the science is conducted appropriately. We need, however, to be more discriminating when we read the reports. There is a further issue, however, which is potentially even more damaging and that concerns *what* they study rather than *how* they study it.

Do Psychology's methods discover anything of value?

In 1867, the American philosopher William James announced that 'perhaps the time has come for psychology to begin to be a science. Some measurements have already been made in the region lying between the physical changes in the nerves and the appearance of consciousness, and more may come of it … Helmholtz and a man named Wundt at Heidelberg are working on it' (James, 1920, p. 119). The 'man named Wundt' was Wilhelm Wundt, and in 1872 he decided to take up James' provocative call-to-arms and devote himself to the *'somewhat suspect borderland between physiology and philosophy'* (cited in Bordogna, 2008, p. 59). He subsequently became known as the father of experimental psychology.

Wundt's aim was not to start a new science but to revitalize philosophy using physiological methods to produce data about the human mind's capabilities. And despite his legendary productivity (Richards, 2002), he did not leave a legacy of either empirical discoveries or theoretical principles. Wundt's first American student, G. Stanley Hall, wrote 'It does not seem to me that he made any epoch-making contributions to psychology, although he will always fill a large place as the first to establish this science on an experimental basis' (Baldwin, 1921).

And here is the challenge, if Wundt did not leave any great 'epoch-making contribution' to psychology, what has happened since? What has psychology achieved in the last 150 years?

Psychology's achievements

If you were asked to list the top five achievements in psychology what would you say? When I've sprung this on colleagues they have come up with suggestions like Attachment Theory or the Multi-stage Memory Model or even cognitive behaviour therapy (CBT). To me, this is not an impressive list and it suggests a horrible truth that for all the bluster about science, for all the fancy equipment and million-pound research grants, we haven't discovered any great new understandings or technologies about our core subject – ourselves.

Yes, we have produced studies and papers that cite and excite our colleagues and, when spun in the right way, can also light up the sofa of the One Show or the Today studio. But does any of it amount to anything more than a hill of beans? The British Psychological Society (BPS) has more than one definition for the subject but on the front page of the website it says 'Psychology is the scientific study of people, the mind and behaviour'. So, what are the headline discoveries about people, mind and behaviour? And do these findings match up to the discoveries of the other sciences?

The discoveries of other sciences

Look at physics, for example, it has split the atom, it has gravity, it has quantum theory, and it has the Hadron Collider and the Higgs boson. It has the Big Bang Theory which offers an explanation of how the universe was formed. Chemistry has the electrochemical series, a classification of all substances in the universe, and biology has evolution, a robust theory of how we came to be here. I could go on. What has psychology got?

'*Psychology is a young science*' we say by way of explanation for the lack of great findings. But 150 years is not that young and there are even younger sciences that have more to show. Electronics has the microchip, genetics has mapped out the human genome and geology has tectonic plates.

The central issue concerns how we develop knowledge in psychology. To start with, other sciences have testable theories whereas psychology has testable hypotheses. What's the difference? Einstein's theory of general relativity was first presented in 1915 and then spectacularly tested in 1919 when light was shown to bend round the sun during a solar eclipse to the amount predicted by the theory. And if we look at the Higgs boson then this was a particle whose existence was predicted by theory. It is an important part of the Standard

Model of particle physics and provided a crucial test of that theory. First proposed in the 1960s, it was finally confirmed to exist in 2013.

What psychological theory produces predictions that can be tested in this way? Or to be even more challenging, what collection of ideas in psychology have we got that we can call a testable theory? What is Psychology's Big Bang?

Scientific products

So, if we haven't got theories then maybe we have transformational products: things that we have invented that have changed lives. Inventions such as the microchip figure highly in any list of inventions that have a major impact on us. Then there is the contraceptive pill which revolutionised women's control of their own fertility and fuelled a massive social change of their position in society.

If you search the Internet for the greatest scientific inventions you get a lot of suggestions such as antiseptics, penicillin, telephones, electric batteries, frozen peas, lasers, sonic screwdrivers, pianos, radar, the internet and my favourite, the non-stick frying pan. In all the lists I browsed I didn't find one invention that you could claim as psychological.

The non-stick frying pan is a great example of an invention that changes lives. It is not revolutionary or even essential but it makes the life of anyone who does any cooking a lot easier. It is commonly believed to have been a bi-product of the space race but the reverse is true and it was a facilitator of it. Not the frying pan of course but the polymer that coats the frying pan which had been invented in the 1930s and used in the Manhattan project to develop the atomic bomb (Elmsley, 1994).

I'm not asking for an invention with the impact of antibiotics or contraceptives or the aeroplane or the combustion engine, but where oh where is our non-stick frying pan? Surely, we have something to match that?

Impeccable trivia

Despite this lack of great findings our research and teaching concentrate on data and techniques. The search for ever-greater scientific rigour has led to research programmes that focus on precisely doing meaningless tasks to come up with idiosyncratic findings and we witness,

> the fetishisation of psychological method, or [...] the impeccable trivia that consume so many journal pages.
>
> (Reicher & Haslam, 2009, p. 469)

Giving psychology away

This chapter reads like a treatise of despair, but I think there is some cause for optimism. Psychology does, in fact, contribute to our everyday life but not in the manner of the other sciences. In his challenging talk to the APA in 1969, George Miller (who we met in chapter 1) seemed to come to the same conclusion.

He argued that psychology has the potential to be one of the most re-volutionary activities ever developed by people. He wrote

> 'if we were ever to achieve substantial progress toward our stated aim – toward the understanding, prediction and control of mental and beha-vioural phenomena – the implications for every aspect of society would make brave men tremble'.
>
> (Miller, 1969, p. 1065)

On the bright side, as pointed out above, psychology rarely lives up to the hype and nothing that it has done so far is very revolutionary.

Miller argued that we are looking in the wrong direction if we are waiting for the great discoveries and applications to appear. He suggested that the revolution will come in how we think of ourselves:

> I believe that the real impact of psychology will be felt, not through the technological products it places in the hands of powerful [people], but through its effects on the public at large, through a new and different public conception of what is humanly possible and humanly desirable.
>
> (Miller, 1969, p. 1066)

The brilliance of psychology is that it provides a secular explanation for our existence, our feelings, thoughts and behaviour. It can help us roll back the fog of superstition, mysticism and religion[1] to provide understandings about ourselves that do not rely on supernatural beings and events. And as the country becomes more and more psychologically literate these understandings have become part of the way we explain the world.

When there is an atrocity or a hate crime then it is psychologists who are commonly asked to comment on it rather than religious leaders. It might well be that psychologists have very little to say or do (see Simon Wessely, 2006; Rose et al., 2002) but at least we are looking to ourselves for answers rather than supernatural beings.

Maybe I'm missing something here. Maybe we do have revolutionary theories and transformational products and I just haven't noticed them So please, just show me our non-stick frying pan.

---

1 The astute reader will notice the author's position here about other sources of knowledge such as religion. I'm not pretending to be objective or to have discovered the truth, but this is my stand-point.

Summary

In this chapter, we have worked our way through some of the controversies that swirl around the way that psychology collects and analyses its data. We have considered whether psychology can be objective and detached from the content of its research, and even whether it should try to achieve this. We have considered how psychology has a tendency to reduce people to widgets in its studies and ignore much of the experience that makes us human. There are also controversies about the quality assurance of research and a challenge to the peer review process that is seen as so important for the progress of science. And finally, there are controversies about the very content of the research and the value it offers to our societies.

On a first read, this can appear as a damning indictment of the subject and its research but the positive spin is that the challenge to these controversies that are going on within the profession and the changes in conduct that are taking place shows how strong and adaptable the subject is. And if you are a psychologist or budding psychologist reading this then take heart from the observation that the great juggernaut of psychology research shows no sign of being derailed yet and the popularity of the subject continues to increase.

3 Is Psychology racist?

Is Psychology racist? The simple and unequivocal answer is yes. I considered writing 'yes' in big enough letters to fill the page and then leaving the rest of the chapter blank. The format of a textbook, however, demands that I provide a reasoned justification for the answer so here goes. Racism is perhaps the strongest fault line in our society and is very difficult to have an honest discussion about. As with all the other controversies in this book, I have a position on this one and, in brief, it is that our society in the UK is structurally racist and we have a lot of work to do to confront this and make our society the haven of freedom and democracy that we sometimes erroneously claim it to be. Below are my best understandings of the issues as they apply to psychology but I am still learning about this and so welcome comments.

We start by looking at racism and psychology before going on to look at some examples of race science in psychology. We then look at two examples of Black psychology that have contributed to our understanding of these issues before asking how psychology can start to address the issue of coloniality.

Racism and Psychology

Defining racism

The more you think about racism the harder it is to define. This is, in part, because the term is used to cover a number of different things and also because there are problems with the concept of race. At one level, racism is expressed and experienced by individuals but that racism is framed and nurtured by the very structures of our society. These structures include the histories we tell, the science we make and the organisations we live and work in.

In the introduction to Memmi's text *Racism* (1999), Steve Martinot offers a summary of racism that has four aspects. First, it insists that a difference exists, either real or imaginary. It can be something about our bodies or beliefs or cultural practices. Second, is the negative valuation on those perceived as seen as being different from the people who are making that valuation. Third, this negative valuation is applied to the whole group. Fourth, this negative valuation becomes the justification for hostility, discrimination and aggression.

DOI: 10.4324/9781003147589-3

Commonly, definitions of racism focus on individual attitudes and behaviours and ignore the structural aspects. The US dictionary Merriam-Webster is changing its definition of racism after receiving a challenge to its current version. A young graduate, Kennedy Mitchum, wrote to Merriam-Webster to suggest that the definition should include a reference to systematic oppression. She made the challenge after receiving some responses to her social media posts that included suggestions that she didn't understand what racism is and using the Merriam-Webster definition as evidence of this (BBC, 2020). Merriam-Webster responded positively to the request and are in the process of changing the definition for the next edition. Definitions matter.

Defining race

The concept of race is problematic but probably best described as being an example of racism. The concept of race that is based on place and physical characteristics emerged in the West around the turn of the 19th century. It emerged for a reason, and that was to distinguish one particular group of people (those inventing the term) from all others, and to provide a rationale and scientific and moral justification for white supremacy. Race does not exist as a biological entity, and although the term is still used it has no scientific meaning.

If races don't exist, should we stop using the term, and stop seeing people as existing within these racial categories? I suggest not yet because these categories have a reality in that people believe in them and these false beliefs negatively impact the lives of so many of our fellow human beings. These beliefs are the essential mortar in the racist structures that make up our society. On a personal level, if I come to the realisation that race does not exist but is, in fact, an oppressive construct, can I stop seeing someone as being Black, for example, and will my nearly seventy years of socialisation into racist thinking just fade away? The answer to this is 'no', so the terms race and racism continue to be part of our narrative even with all the contradictions they raise. Below, we look at how psychology has defined and contributed to narrative.

Racism in the UK

Racism is not something that is out there and something that other people do. It is part of the fabric of our society. In the UK, we have a narrative that largely sees us as morally superior as exemplified in our fight against fascism during the Second World War (1939–1945), and as making major gifts to human development (football, Shakespeare, civility). A cursory read of history, however, gives another and much less pleasant side to this story.

Our society in the UK developed its wealth and power through the subjugation and exploitation of peoples in other parts of the world over a period of several hundred years. Millions of people were enslaved and transported across the globe to further the financial interests of Europeans and, in particular, the British. These atrocities barely make a footnote in the narrative of the UK that we commonly bask in. Next time, you go to a stately home or a historical building maybe take the time to reflect where the wealth came from to build it.

The consequences of these social and political upheavals are still playing out, and the world we live in favours some groups over others. One very striking aspect of this can be seen in the racist attitudes and structures that are part of our lives, and are so embedded that they are often unseen by the majority of people (mainly because they are not disadvantaged by them). As a quick example, think back to when you were in school and count up how many of the staff who taught you were people of colour, and how many people of colour were there in the school management? The recent pandemic is another example, with the Office for National Statistics reporting that Black and Asian people were between 2 and 3 times more likely to die than white people, illustrating the structural disadvantages these people experience (Office for National Statistics, 2021). The NHS has been found to be racist in its dealings with its own staff and also patients from historically marginalised groups, for example, the way it delivers treatment to people with sickle cell disease (Sky News, 2021).

Is psychology immune from this? Is psychology research racist? The simple answers to these questions are a) no and b) yes.[1] It is perhaps a good idea to explore this to see in what ways psychology is racist and what we can do to start to address this. Psychology has a history of asking questions that have promoted racist attitudes and behaviours, and it continues to frame its question within a white, European context. Some examples of this are described later in the chapter.

Psychology is in an excellent position, however, to promote and lead discussion of issues around racism and help in the emancipation of all disadvantaged people. This is not easy stuff though as we have to work through the many layers of our socialisation. If you are interested in reading more about these issues then I suggest *White Fragility* by Robin DiAngelo and *Discourse on Colonialism* by Aimé Césaire.

Racism in universities

Many people are offended and upset to have their behaviour challenged as being racist and see racism as being a feature of other people and not themselves. The arbitrary division of the world into racists and non-racists is not helpful as it prevents us from reflecting on our own behaviour and masks the behaviours that occur in liberal institutions like universities that position themselves as anti-racist. These institutions have clear evidence of racism in their student achievement data and also their staff recruitment. Every twenty years or so a new report highlights the problems, there are predictable expressions of shock and horror but no action to bring about change. The

---

1 It is also important to add that psychology has issues to deal with around sexism and other discriminatory behaviours.

chances for a career in academia are dramatically reduced for Black staff compared to their white colleagues (BBC, 2021a).

Data from UK universities show that students from historically marginalised groups are less likely to get good degrees (usually defined as a 1st or 2.1) and are less likely to progress on their courses. The data are usually collected using the category of 'Black, Asian, Minoritised Ethnic (BAME)' so I'll use this term here. These data were reviewed by Jankowski who showed that BAME students are 13% less likely to be awarded a high-degree classification, are less likely to be employed after graduating, and earn significantly less than their White graduating peers. BAME students also report racist harassment on campus, isolation and receiving limited support from staff (Jankowski, 2021).

Universities commonly refer to the disparities in student outcomes as an achievement gap though it would be better termed as an ignorance gap (Bell, 2021). The term 'achievement gap' puts the focus on the individual students and looks to explain why they don't do as well as their white co-students. The better question is to look at what the staff and the university structures are doing that holds back the achievement of these students (the ignorance of these staff and structures). I know from unpublished data from my own university that these differences in performance do not occur on all courses or in all modules, so it is possible to make changes to remove the barriers to success in all students.

To make the changes that will remove the barriers requires us to challenge ourselves and our colleagues and to recognise the racism that lies deep within the way we construct and deliver courses. It is also necessary for managers to review their recruitment procedures to address the relatively low level of staff and re-search students from historically marginalised groups. You can appreciate that this is very controversial and will meet with a lot of denial and resistance.

Racism in the professions

Structural racism is not confined to universities but is also present in the psychology profession. Psychologists are employed in education, the prison service, the health service and beyond. All of these professions report a low proportion of staff from the historically marginalised groups, and difficulties in dealing with issues of race. The people these professionals deal with such as children excluded from schools, people with mental health difficulties and people confined to prisons, disproportionately come from these historically marginalised groups. The issues for the professions are starting to be discussed (Gill, 2020; Fazir-Short, 2020), as are the issues for counselling psychology (Charura & Lago, 2021) and clinical psychology (Memon et al., 2016), but given how long there has been literature on this the current state of the psychology professions is difficult to excuse.

The literature has been available for a long time. In 1976, Robert V. Guthrie (1998) published the first edition of *Even the Rat was White: A Historical View of Psychology* which described the traditions of race science in psychology that had been used to legitimise the oppression of Black people in the United States (and beyond). The book also showcased the work of Black psychologists who then, and now, were not given the prominence and respect their work warranted. We look at the work of Kenneth and Mamie Clark below. The second edition published in 1998 reviews progress since publication of the first edition and discusses the new challenges for Black psychologists. Guthrie argues that the 'myth of mental measurement' and eugenicist philosophy continue to exist and create negative stereotypes of oppressed peoples. We explore this myth of measurement in the next chapter.

The literature on the racist nature of psychiatric diagnosis has also been available for years. Littlewood and Lipsedge wrote their first edition of their classic text *Aliens and Alienists* in 1982 in which they outlined the links between racism, psychological ill health and the inadequate treatment of patients from historically marginalised groups (see Littlewood and Lipsedge, 1997). We will also explore some of the issues around diagnosis in the next chapter.

Racism in the literature

In chapter 2, we looked at how psychology homogenises the people it studies and effectively ignores their individual experiences. One effect of this is to whitewash the data so that the default is about the dominant white communities. This has been reflected in textbooks for many years. An analysis of introductory textbooks by Smith and Bond (1993) found that they mainly cited work by researchers from America. In a fairly standard American text by Baron and Byrne (1991) 94% of the 1,700 studies mentioned were in fact from America. In a British text (Hewstone et al., 1988), about 66% of the studies were American, 32% were European and under 2% came from the rest of the world.

A study of the images in psychology textbooks (Collins & Hebert, 2008) found significantly more images of males than females and a high preponderance of white people featured in the images. Jankowski and colleagues (2017) describe how most of our journals are edited by Westerners, written by Westerners and use Westerners as participants. They examined their own teaching and after coding the ethnicity, nationality and gender of every author of every reading they set from the module handbooks of their psychology course discovered that of the 215 readings they set, written by 380 authors, 96% were white, 99% were Western and 64% were male. The authors note that their own modules were no better than any other in this regard. The disarming honesty of the authors and willingness to address this is in stark contrast to the general air of defensiveness that many of us display when challenged.

Summary

Racism runs through the institutions of our society and also through psychology. It continues to harm the lives of many people. The issues are well documented but there has been little action to bring about meaningful change. Psychology also has a history of tolerating race science and we move on to that in the next section.

Examples of race science in Psychology

Galton and race science

In 1859, Darwin's *Origin of Species* was published and changed the way that see the development of life on our planet. It heralds the start of our understanding about evolution and a new understanding of what it means to be human. It also heralds the start of a new chapter in race science. Darwin's work was extrapolated to look at perceived differences between people and, in particular, justify white domination. This extrapolation tried to argue that White people were further evolved than other peoples and that their domination and subjugation of these people which had been achieved through military might was in fact an indication of their biological superiority. These beliefs saw the start of individual differences as a field of study in psychology.

The study of individual differences can be traced back to the work of Francis Galton who was Darwin's nephew. Galton is credited with developing a staggering range of techniques and concepts (see Fancher 1996) including, self-report questionnaires, twin studies, scatterplots and statistics. Galton's work was driven by one major concern – how we can best manipulate the forces of evolution to the advantage of the human race. The idea is expressed in his book *Hereditary Genius*,

> As it is easy ... to obtain by careful selection a permanent breed of dogs or horses gifted with peculiar powers of running, or of doing anything else, so would it be quite practicable to produce a highly-gifted race of men by judicious marriages during several consecutive generations.
>
> (Galton, 1869, reproduced in Fancher 1990, p. 228)

He went on to found a discipline he named Eugenics which was aimed at improving his race through selective breeding. And here is the problem at the heart of mental testing from the beginning until today, the focus on perceived differences between groups of people and, in particular, between White people and peoples from historically marginalised communities. Galton wasn't interested in the human race but the White race. For example, Galton wrote,

> There exists a sentiment for the most part quite unreasonable against the gradual extinction of an inferior race.
>
> (Francis Galton, 1883, cited in Rose et al., 1984, p. 30)

In his text *Hereditary Genius*, Galton writes a chapter on 'The comparative worth of different races'. You'll not be surprised to hear that white Europeans come out as the pinnacle of development and other peoples are presented on a sliding scale of inferiority.

Galton and his colleague Karl Pearson developed statistical techniques that would create evidence to support their views. The tools of psychometrics and individual differences are rooted in white supremacy and eugenics. Despite this, Galton's work, and that of many other supporters of race science is commonly presented without mention of this aspect to the work.

Race science flourished during the early part of the 20th century and we look at a specific example when we consider intelligence testing in the next chapter. Political events, however, such as the Second World War made eugenic ideas less acceptable and the Civil Rights Movement in the United States, and the challenge to colonialism across the world started to chip away at the mainstream expression of White supremacy. However, race science didn't go away, it just changed its form.

Scientific racism

In 1990, the flagship journal of the British Psychological Society, *The Psychologist* published an article by Philippe Rushton (1990). In this article, Rushton proposed a modern theory of 'racial differences' that once again attempted to put forward an evolutionary explanation. There are a number of scientific and political objections to this approach which we have covered above.

Despite the obvious theoretical, practical and political problems with writing about race differences, The Psychologist chose to publish the article by Rushton (1990) which put forward an academically shallow but openly racist set of ideas. It is hard to explain just how poor the data is and, indeed, how offensive it is. The first major problem with the article is the division of the world's people into three races. The justification for this is slight if not non-existent. These 'data' are expressed in tabular form using terms such as low, medium and high. For example, lifespan is assessed as 'high' or 'low' in Rushton's racial categories. The most likely explanation for these differences is the economic disadvantage that exists in some countries, especially those whose wealth is still being plundered by large multinational companies based in the West. Another item in the table refers to the age of first intercourse. This seems a strange item to have in the table for two reasons, first because it does not seem to make sense (what does it mean to have a 'slow age of first intercourse'?), and second because it appears to be a pointless observation. It is there, however, because of the underlying idea behind the work, and that is the idea of neoteny.

Neoteny is the extension in childhood that evolution has given human beings. Most animals are born with their brains fully formed or fairly nearly formed. The chimpanzee has the greatest post-birth development but that stops after 9 months. Human brains, however, continue to develop until we are about 20 years old. This is what gives us our adaptability. The argument that Rushton made was that some races have a longer childhood than others and are, therefore, further down the evolutionary road. This is a re-working of Galton's attempts to provide a scientific justification for white supremacy. These scientific arguments do not stand up to scrutiny, though this has not stopped their popularisation.

What is most remarkable about the Rushton story is not that some people put forward racist views attached to bogus science, but that a prestigious journal should choose to publish it. And this is the rub. We can define ourselves by our attitudes and our behaviour, but we need to include in this self-definition the attitudes and behaviours that we are prepared to tolerate in others. And as psychologists, what sort of attitudes and ideas are we prepared to accept in the name of free speech, in this case, racist ones?

I have been very selective with the above examples to try and give a flavour of the ideas that have been presented in the tradition of scientific racism. If you want to read more about this, I recommend *'Race', Racism and Psychology,* by Graham Richards (2012). We move on to look at how psychology has looked at race issues.

The study of prejudice

Prejudice has been of particular interest to social psychologists. Many textbooks carry discussions of it and some of the studies are amongst the most well-known of psychological investigations and theories. Among the important studies are the work of Adorno et al. (1950) on the authoritarian personality, the work of Sherif (1956) on the conflict theory of prejudice, and the work of Tajfel (1970) on minimal groups. One feature that united all this work was that it looked at the person who is prejudiced and tried to explain their behaviour.

A major issue with the study of prejudice in psychology is that it is portrayed as an individual issue and one that is mainly a matter of attitude. Racism has been narrowed down to an act by a (bad) person and removed from the context of the society in which it has been nurtured. One of the concepts that was explored in this work was ethnocentrism which sees group membership as an inevitable part of social interaction and that the groups we belong to are on a sliding scale from sports team affiliation through to ethnicity. This idea ignores the nature of racism and its creation in its current form by white supremacist Europeans. It largely ignores or denies the experiences that are expressed by people from traditionally marginalized groups.

Cross-cultural studies

Psychology has a tradition of looking at people from a range of cultures. This work is often referred to as cross-cultural studies. Although it provides a wider picture of human behaviour and experience than can be gained by just looking at our own culture there are some problems with this approach, especially as it is presented in textbooks. The people from cultures other than the West are sometimes presented as quite exotic: strange people from strange countries doing strange things. They are often described in a way that compares them against some idea of a Western norm.

One of the issues to consider is the language we use to describe people and their behaviour. We might say that someone belongs to a group, or a culture or a nation or a tribe. Each of these terms carries a number of assumptions with it. It is hard to imagine a context where we would describe someone from Yorkshire as belonging to a tribe, but we might use that term to describe someone from Africa. Language, as we have already seen, matters.

Summary

The above is a very selective look at psychology and how it has dealt with issues of race and racism. It is not meant to be a full account, but to illustrate how openly racist ideas have been tolerated within Psychology. And how some of the attempts to explore the issue of racism have taken the perspective of the researchers and sought to ignore or deny the experience of marginalized and disadvantaged people. It is, perhaps, important to point out that in the UK there is also a tradition of anti-racist psychologists (see Richards, 2012).

Studies in self and identity

In this section, I outline two examples of the work on self and identity that I believe contribute to our understanding of racism in psychology. I start with a series of studies in social psychology by Clark and Clark (1939, 1947, 1950) though as you will see in the following work by Nobles, it is not without its criticism.

Concepts of self

Very rarely in psychology does a piece of research have a dramatic, enduring positive impact on a nation. The work of Clark and Clark is an example of one that did. In 1939, Clark and Clark first reported their work on racial identification and preference in Black US children. They were interested in how racial awareness developed and devised a novel test using dolls with different skin colours. Clark and Clark (1947) found that Black children preferred White dolls and rejected Black dolls when asked to choose which were nice, which looked bad, which they would like to play with and which were a nice colour. This suggested that Black children had negative attitudes towards themselves and their cultural background.

The political context to these studies was the US social policy towards Black people. By the start of the 20th century, slavery had been banned but new ways to oppress people had been created. Under a court ruling passed in 1896, it became legal to create a segregated society under the principle of 'separate but equal' and many parts of the United States used this principle to have separate buses, drinking fountains and schools for Black and White people. You will not be surprised to know that the facilities for Black people were very far from equal and a legal battle was fought against the 'separate but equal' court ruling.

As they went from state to state challenging the policy of segregated education Clark and Clark repeated their studies in each state and came to the same conclusions. They were able to show scientifically something that seems so obvious today – if you treat someone with disrespect for long enough they end up internalising that disrespect. The anti-segregation cases were eventually taken to the Supreme Court of the United States (the highest court in the country) and the Clarks prepared evidence on the effects of segregation. The Supreme Court acknowledged the work presented by Clark and Clark noting the following about the effects of segregation on Black children:

> To separate them from others of similar age and qualifications solely because of their race generates a feeling of inferiority as to their status in the community that may affect their hearts and minds in a way unlikely ever to be undone....
>
> (Clark in O'Connell & Russo, 2001, p. 271)

On May 17th, 1954 (*Brown vs Topeka Board of Education*), the principle of 'separate but equal' was ruled illegal.

At first glance, the doll studies of Clark and Clark seem quite slight but don't be misled here. Big ideas can sometimes be demonstrated with relatively simple studies, and Clark and Clark were able to make some profound statements about self-identity from their studies. The results of this speeded up the emancipation of Black people in the United States and so can reasonably be said to be one of psychology's most important studies of the 20th century, though you don't see it featured in many UK textbooks.

After the original doll studies were published Mamie Phipps Clark continued her work at Columbia University where, in 1943, she became the first African-American woman and the second African-American (after her husband Kenneth Clark) in the University's history to receive a psychology doctorate. However, even after her ground-breaking work Phipps Clark had difficulty finding work as a psychologist. She described her frustration:

> Although my husband had earlier secured a teaching position at the City College of New York, following my graduation it soon became apparent to me that a black female with a Ph.D. in psychology was an unwanted anomaly in New York City in the early 1940's.
>
> (O'Connell & Russo, 2001, p. 271)

Mamie Phipps Clark and Kenneth Clark had to struggle against racism all their professional lives and it is disappointing but perhaps not surprising that their work still does not receive much attention today. An attempt to correct this was made in 2001 when the American Psychological Association sponsored a conference on race and identity that led to a book on the legacy of Kenneth Clark (Philogene, 2004).

A Girl Like Me

This might all seem like a piece of history as you read the above but there is a recent addition to the story. In 2005, a young Black filmmaker, Kiri Davis, repeated Clark's experiment in New York. You can see this remarkable study called *A Girl Like Me* on YouTube.

Scientific colonialism

In Western culture, and therefore also Western psychology, we have an idea that people are separate individuals who stand completely alone. In psychology, we talk about the self-concept which refers to the way I perceive myself as being quite unique from, and unconnected to any other person. This philosophy of the self is not held by all cultures. A powerful critique of this approach was provided by Wade Nobles (1976).

Nobles begins by observing that in social science, the scientist commonly occupies a position of economic, psychological and political superiority over the people they are studying. As such their position is very similar to that of the colonist and their subject people. In the article, he goes on to explore how scientific colonialism impacts our understanding of peoples who are not European. He summarises this in Table 3.1.

Nobles goes on to critique the work on Black identity (including the doll studies) because the research questions are framed within the colonial context and so they can only come up with a limited set of possible answers. He argues that to understand research we need to know the philosophical and theoretical assumptions that underpin it.

Afrocentrism

Nobles observes that the general characteristics of Western philosophy are different from those of African philosophy. As a result, any data that concerns

Table 3.1 Comparative colonialisms (from Nobles, 1976)

	Political colonialism	*Scientific colonialism*
1. Removal of Wealth	Exportation of raw materials and wealth from colonies for the purpose of 'processing' it into manufactured wealth and/or goods.	Exporting raw data from a community for the purpose of 'processing' it into manufactured goods (i.e., books, articles, wealth, etc.)
2. Right of Access and Claim	Colonial Power believes it has the right of access and use for its own benefit anything belonging to the colonized people.	Colonial Power believes it has the right of access and use for its own access to any data.
3. External Power Base	The center of power and control over the colonized is located outside of the colony itself. source and any information belonging to the subject population.	The center of knowledge and information about a people or community located outside of the community or people themselves.

African peoples but is processed in the West is distorted by Western as-sumptions. For example, two themes in Western science are (i) survival of the fittest and (ii) control over nature. Nobles suggests that these themes are re-flected in the Western emphasis on competition, individual rights, in-dependence and separateness. In psychology, this has led to an emphasis on individuality, uniqueness and individual differences.

By contrast, the themes of the African world view, according to Nobles, are (i) survival of the people and (ii) oneness with nature. The contrast with Western values could not be greater. The group are more important than the individual and the environment is there to be adjusted to rather than changed. These themes are reflected in the African values of co-operation, inter-dependence and collective responsibility. The psychological emphasis would then be on commonality, groupness and similarity. The differences in the two approaches are summarised in Figure 3.1.

Nobles writes,

> The effects of these two different world-views on the understanding of Black self-concept is critical. The nature of the "processing" of data regarding Black people and our self-conceptions was, in fact, filtered through the European world-view and to the extent that Black people are an African people, the "process" has significantly distorted the validity of Black self-conception.
>
> (pp. 19–20)

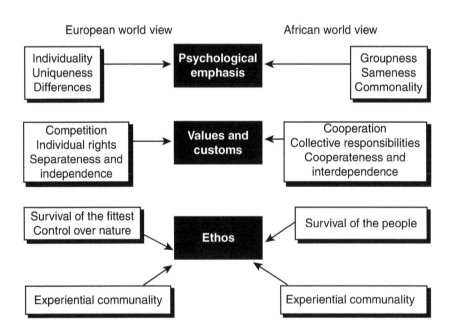

Figure 3.1 Comparative world-view schematic (from Nobles 1976).

Nobles argued that in understanding the traditional African concept of self we must consider the belief that 'I am because We are, and because We are therefore I am'. A person's self-definition is dependent on the definition of the people. Therefore, if we try and describe all people using the Western ideas about self-concept we will fail to see the social links and understandings that many people have in cultures other than the West.

Summary

The pioneering work of Clark and Clark forced a new voice into the consciousness of US psychology and demonstrated the political effect that psychology can have. They did this within the context of individual differences, and as Nobles points out, there is a limit to where this approach can go as it is framed by all the assumptions of Western (and hence racist) psychology. Nobles' work was part of Black Psychology movement that sought to create a new framework for our understandings of people. More recently, the focus has shifted to understanding the colonial nature of Western thought, and hence psychological thought, and exploring how we can decolonise psychology and, indeed, our society.

Decolonising psychology

Let's start with some uncomfortable truths. The colonial past of the UK is a horror story. I know that when it is presented in dramas it is usually seen as amusing or an exotic backdrop to a family psychodrama about colonists, but the truth is actually brutal. The European colonies enslaved millions, transported them across the world and created conditions that caused unimaginable destruction, suffering and death. They developed the techniques for dominating people that we now see as the hallmarks of fascism. The British colonists were particularly inventive at this. Our nation looks back fondly to the Second World War with pride and without any sense of shame as if this was our finest hour. Much of the war, however, took place outside of Europe and was not defending the country but maintaining the empire.

For example, allied troops were fighting in Myanmar (then known by its colonial name of Burma), not for democracy within that country but to maintain British control. A control that gave access to the natural resources of rubies and teak oil. At its height, over one million people were fighting under the Union Jack in Burma. They were not fighting for democracy, they were fighting against it. They were not fighting against fascism, they were fighting to maintain fascist control over the colonies.

During that same conflict, Bengal experienced a massive famine that killed over three million people. This is the only famine in modern Indian history not to come about from drought. The catastrophe was man-made and I use that gendered term deliberately because it was made by a man and that man was Winston Churchill. The British War Cabinet was repeatedly warned about the risks of overusing resources from India and continued to export rice from the country even as the famine raged (The Guardian, 2019). The occupying colonists also confiscated boats and rice from coastal areas in Bengal to deny resources to the Japanese army in case they invaded (they didn't). Churchill has been quoted as blaming the famine on the fact Indians were 'breeding like rabbits', and asking how, if the shortages were so bad, Mahatma Gandhi was still alive.

The above examples show the disregard that the empire showed towards the people it subjugated. It is possible to fill book after book with this story and the many outrages of the colonialists. The enduring problem is that our society (and the societies of other colonial powers) do not face up to the historic actions of their governments and hence do not recognise the enduring suffering that exists even when much of the structure of the empire has been dismantled. In a society that basks in the moral superiority of a war that in fact maintained fascist control around the world rather than eliminating it, you will observe that it is near impossible to have a frank discussion about decolonising our society and decolonising psychology.

One of the key issues for psychology is to try and understand,

> ... the mentality of a people that could continue for over 300 years to kidnap an estimated 50 million youth and young adults from Africa, transport them across the Atlantic with about half dying unable to withstand the inhumanity of the passage, and enslave them as animals.
>
> (Linda James–Myers, 1988)

Decolonising basics

Decolonising has become a buzzword at the time of writing but it is not well understood in psychology. Some responses that are badged as decolonising in education deal with issues such as diversifying the curriculum so that it includes work from psychologists other than mainstream Western psychology. This review of the curriculum adds breadth and some different voices and is a welcome change. This work takes considerable effort and thought and is a major challenge to the current psychology curriculum. However, it does not start to address the underlying issues of colonialism.

At a more superficial level, texts and promotional materials are reviewed so that they have images that reflect the diversity that exists in our society. The fact that we have to have committees reviewing this material and that, even then, there are many fails shows how far there is to go.

One of the challenges to colonial influences is to revisit and, commonly, remove the statues and artifacts of the colonialists. The removal of the statue of slave trader Edward Colson from its place in the heart of Bristol is a good example though the statue has subsequently been fished out of the dock it was thrown into. And then, there is Cecil Rhodes who was a Victorian colonialist whose activities caused untold suffering in southern Africa and systematically plundered the wealth of that region. Despite this, Oxford University resists any attempts to remove the statue of Rhodes (BBC, 2021b).

We remove statuses and traces of people and events that we now understand to be brutal, oppressive, but our society makes an exception for colonialists even though there is clear evidence of their crimes against humanity. Imagine a university keeping its statue of Jimmy Saville. What level of outrage would there be? In 1877 Rhodes wrote, 'I contend that we are the first race in the world, and that the more of the world we inhabit the better it is for the human race. I contend that every acre added to our territory means the birth of more of the English race who otherwise would not be brought into existence' (cited on Wikipedia). If our institutions protect statues for white supremacists, the work of decolonists is going to be very difficult. Putting a few happy smiling faces on the front of a university prospectus is not going to cut it.

But what has this to do with psychology I hear you ask? The examples here concern institutions such as Oxford University and not the discipline of psychology. My view is that the statues create a climate of acceptance for racist ideas and that this exists within psychology as well. Every person that enters into Oriel College, Oxford, walks under a statue of a white supremacist whose place there is fiercely protected by the University. In psychology, we ask students to accept the work of white supremacists such as Pearson and Spearman without comment. Until 2021, the highest award of the British Psychological Society was the Spearman Award. The statistical tests named after them were designed to show the superiority of white British people over all others. This process of categorising and ranking people is still the main activity of the field of individual differences.

Decolonial strategies in psychology

As I hope I have indicated above, colonial thinking goes very deep. One of the key ideas of decolonial thinking is that the violence of colonialism was not confined to a period of history but persists today in coloniality which we define as ways of knowing, power and being, formed during colonial occupation, that persist after the end of colonial rule (Gómez-Ordóñez et al. 2021). Adding some new images and a handful of new studies to existing materials and curricula will not move us on very far.

Much of the knowledge in psychology is based on a narrow view of humanity that focuses on the behaviour and experience of WEIRD (Western, Educated, Industrialised, Rich, and allegedly Democratic) people. The behaviour and experience of these WEIRD people have come to be seen as the norms against which everything is judged. One way to challenge this colonial thinking is to assert the value of other ways of being, and de-normalise the WEIRD ways of being.

Decolonial psychologists have pointed us towards strategies that can start us moving in a decolonial direction. My colleague Deanne Bell suggests four moves we can make (Bell, 2020),

1   Decolonise knowledge production. This means doing research that is participatory, as opposed to doing research where the researcher with all of that power and status goes in and extracts knowledge from people.
2   Decolonise teaching, learning and training. The model we currently use is of the expert who gives the accepted knowledge to a passive student group. This model does not ask students to truly critically engage with knowledge and does not include their experience of social reality into the discussion.
3   Decolonise practice. As outlined above, the professions of psychology and our institutions such as the NHS have problems with institutional racism. One way to start to understand and deal with this is to invite these institutions to do participatory research in those places.
4   Decolonise social policy. This requires us to invite everybody who's part of the experience of coloniality into participating in the discussions about it. The standard response is to engage consultants but this is not participatory because it's the ones with power who set the questions, who set the terms.

There is so much to write about decolonising psychology and I have only scratched the surface here. I also have to add that I have a lot to learn about this work. Decolonial psychologists are working to inform colleagues and to facilitate the decolonial process. Given everything else in this chapter, you will understand that theirs is a minority voice and they experience resistance and denial. In my experience, however, they remain remarkably positive.

Summary

Decolonising psychology is a non-trivial task and has to take place within a culture that views its colonial past as its gift to the world rather than the focus for 400 years of subjugation and exploitation. The information is out there to facilitate decolonisation. Psychology can choose to explore this or not.

4 Why are we still categorising and quantifying people?

> **Caesar**: Let me have men about me that are fat,
> Sleek-headed men and such as sleep a-nights.
> Yond Cassius has a lean and hungry look,
> He thinks too much; such men are dangerous.
>
> (Julius Caesar, Act 1, Scene 2, 190–195)

Shakespeare puts words in Caesar's mouth that show his belief that our personality can be read by observing our appearance. This connection of body type to personality has a history back to ancient Greece and probably beyond. We still use all manner of folk methods today to categorise people by observing how they look, what they do and what they say. When we meet someone new we look for familiar characteristics and feel comfortable when we observe that they have behaviours and attitudes in common with other people we have met. We can categorise them. Of course, when we do this we massively simplify the judgement of the other person and miss out so much of their individuality, and we are often wrong. Categorising is a useful shorthand for dealing with everyday life, and it's useful for biological studies, but is it the best way for psychology to explore human behaviour and experience?

The controversies we are dealing with in this chapter concern the value of psychometric testing and the value of diagnostic categories. Do they add to our understanding of people or diminish it? And by categorising and quantifying people do we understand or ignore the experience and behaviour of individuals and groups? We start by looking at the nuts and bolts of psychometric testing before going on to look at how they are used to investigate personality. The final section of the chapter looks at diagnosis and (spoiler alert) how these diagnoses obscure rather than illuminate the experiences of mental distress.

Psychometric testing

Psychometric testing is psychology's big idea and also its biggest moneymaker. Think of all the surveys and tests you have taken. These tests are used to allocate people to jobs, to match them up for relationships, to describe their

DOI: 10.4324/9781003147589-4

personalities, to create diagnoses and so much more. Many of these tests use tick-box questionnaires to get their data, but how meaningful are these data? In this first section, we look at the technology of testing to gain an appreciation of what these tests are measuring.

There are a number of issues to consider including,

- Practical issues: Do the tests give accurate and consistent results? Do the complex statistical procedures illuminate or disguise what is going on?
- Theoretical issues: Do the tests measure underlying psychological qualities? For example, is there such a quality as psychopathy and can it be measured by a tick-box test?
- Political and philosophical issues: Can the tests be used to look at differences between groups of people, for example, different social classes, or the differences between men and women? What are the consequences for our view of humanity if we categorise and quantify people?

The term psychometric means 'measuring the mind', though many psychometricians would be very uncomfortable with a term such as 'mind'. A psychological test is a task or set of tasks that can be given in a standard format to an individual, and which produce a score that can be represented as a number (or a category). It can involve almost any activity, though most commonly, for reasons of practicality, it involves filling in a questionnaire. Tests are used to measure cognitive functions (e.g., IQ tests), personality (e.g., Costa and McCrae's Big Five, see below), mood (e.g., the Beck Depression Inventory), attitudes (e.g., political opinion polls), aptitude for various jobs (e.g., the Comprehensive Ability Battery), illness behaviour (e.g., the McGill Pain Inventory), and many other qualities. Psychometric tests are extensively used in everyday life and you are likely to come into contact with them on a regular basis.

Performance and competence

One of the first issues to consider is the distinction between performance and competence. Performance is what you actually do, and competence is what you are capable of. It is a common experience of students that their teachers say 'you have the ability, but you are not doing the work'. They mean that the reason you got a Grade E in your examinations was due to poor performance and not poor ability (competence). Any test we give to someone can only measure their performance on that test at that time, and not their competence or underlying characteristics. We can only infer their competence from that performance. So when we are measuring intelligence, we are, in fact, measuring *performance* on the particular test and not the underlying *intellectual competence*. We come back to this in the next chapter.

The problem that arises when we interpret the results of a test is the many factors that affect performance. These factors include language, context and motivation. If we are looking at cognitive concepts like intelligence, then the language we use for the questions, the cultural baggage of the questions and the individual's motivation to succeed will all have an effect on the performance. If we are looking at personality tests or clinical tests they will be affected by a self-serving bias to present yourself in a good light and by your motivation to answer honestly. This means that we are not getting a full or accurate picture from these tests.

Measuring people

To measure something you have to compare it against something else. If we are measuring the length of a table, it is easy because we can use a ruler, but if we are measuring people what can we use? There are three ways in which we can use tests to measure people;

1   Direct measurement: Where we use a physical measure such as grip strength or reaction time. Although these measures can be useful, there are only a limited number of direct measures we can make of people.
2   Criterion-referenced measurement: Where we compare the performance of an individual against an ideal performance.
3   Norm-referenced measurement: Where we compare the performance of an individual against the performance of other people, most commonly the peer group. This is far and away from the most common way of using psychological tests.

Norm referencing creates an average performance for comparison. By default, this is seen as the ideal performance or even the normal behaviour. Imagine a measure of racism, however, and in a society with widespread institutional racism (and I believe this describes the UK), then racist responses will be the average and will come to be seen as normal or even ideal by the scale.

Test reliability

If we are using a psychometric test, we need to know whether it will give us a consistent result. So if we give someone the test on a Wednesday afternoon, we hope to get the same results as if we had given the test on Friday morning. It would remarkable if we got exactly the same result because all forms of measurement have an element of error in them, but we hope this error is relatively small. Psychologists use a number of techniques for assessing reliability including

1   *Test–retest*: In this case, we administer the test on two occasions and compare the scores using a correlation technique.

Test–retest reliability is affected by a number of factors including

a   Changes in participants, for example, if we leave a gap of three months the test and the re-test of an IQ test, we can reasonably expect children to develop their intellectual skills in that time, and since children develop at different rates their rank order will also change during that time. This will reduce the test–retest reliability calculation.

b   Measurement error, for example, changes in mood brought about by a hangover for one administration of the test, poor test instructions so the participants do not grasp what is required, and guessing, which people always do but produces a degree of unreliability in the scores.

c   Other factors, for example, if the time gap between the two test times is very brief then the participants are likely to remember their answers, or if the questions are very easy then you will get a high-reliability value because the participants get them nearly all right on both occasions.

2. Internal consistency reliability: in this case, we compare two parts of the test to see how similar the scores are.

Before the arrival of desktop computers, the most common way to calculate internal consistency was through split-half reliability. This method correlates the response to half the items (e.g., the odd-numbered items) to the other items (the even-numbered items). This gives a rough approximation of the reliability value though a number of corrections are made to the scores to take account of such things as test length (the longer the test the greater the reliability, so if you split the test into two you inevitably reduce the reliability score). A more sophisticated version of the split halves technique looks at all the possible split halves and gives a value of reliability called co-efficient alpha. This makes an estimate of the amount of error in the test and hence what the 'true' score would be without any error. It then compares your score with this 'true' score to give a measure of reliability.

The above reliability techniques have serious errors in them because they make assumptions about the data that are rarely appropriate (Shevlin, 1995: Shevlin & Miles, 1998). Psychometricians, therefore, use more complex measures of reliability that use a similar principle to that used by co-efficient alpha but do not make so many assumptions about the data. If you are interested in the technology of testing then you should refer to Kline, (1991), or Kaplan & Saccuzzo (1993).

We can take two general points from the above, first that there are a number of statistical controversies in psychometrics about how to evaluate the data. Second, we can see that measurement always contains error, but that psychologists have been developing statistical tools for over one hundred years to reduce this error, and the whole testing business is statistically very sophisticated. As a result, there are a number of reliable psychometric tests that are used to measure a wide range of psychological variables. But what are they really measuring?

Test validity

A test is said to be valid if it measures what it claims to measure. So, we consider whether a depression scale measures depression and whether an IQ test measures intelligence. This is not as obvious as it sounds, and it is a complex process to measure this validity.

There are a number of types of validity but perhaps the most important is construct validity. If a test has construct validity it matches up with a psychological concept or theory. If a test has construct validity then the following should occur,

a   the scores of the test should correlate with other tests of the same psychological quality.
b   the scores of the test should not correlate with tests of different psychological qualities.
c   the scores of the test should predict future performance.
d   the test items should have some connection to the appropriate psychological theory.

Psychometricians go to great lengths to establish the validity of their tests. Many of these tests, however, continue to attract controversy about what they actually measure, as you'll see below.

Standardisation

The idea of standardisation rests on the principle that abilities, both mental and physical, are distributed throughout a population according to a normal distribution curve (see chapter 2). This curve describes a set of scores where a few people obtain extreme high scores, a few people obtain extreme low scores, and most people score around the average. If we assume that the scores are normally distributed then we can make judgements about the performance of an individual using the statistics of standard deviation and z-scores.

Standardising a test involves establishing how the scores of this test are distributed among the population, and making sure that the test, if administered to enough people, will produce a normal distribution. This involves testing large numbers of people and establishing what the normal scores for those types of people might be. From this, it is possible to develop population norms, which identify what would be an average score, what would be above-average, and what would be below-average; so standardisation, at least in theory, allows us to judge how typical, or uncommon, someone's result is.

Impact of Events Scale (IES-R)

Let's briefly look at an example of a psychometric test. A commonly used test to assess distress caused by traumatic events is the Impact of Events Scale (see Weiss & Marmar, 1996). In its revised form, it has 22 items (statements) that are rated on a 5 point scale from 0 to 4. As defined by the DSM (see the section below on diagnosis), the condition of post-traumatic stress disorder (PTSD) has three main groups of symptoms: re-experiencing phenomena (e.g., recurrent and intrusive distressing memories of the traumatic event or situation), avoidance or numbing reactions (such as efforts to avoid the thoughts or feelings associated with the trauma, and feeling of detached or estranged from other people) and symptoms of increased arousal (such as difficulty in staying asleep, irritability and outbursts of anger). The IES-R has three sub-scales that map onto these three groups of symptoms.

It is possible to access the test online[1] and to self-administer it and to self-diagnose. The test asks you to 'read each item, and then indicate how distressing each difficulty has been for you DURING THE PAST SEVEN DAYS'. The scale is 0 = not at all; 1 = a little, 2 = moderately, 3 = quite a bit, 4 = extremely. The statements include 'I had trouble staying asleep' and 'I thought about it when I didn't mean to'. You respond to all 22 items and then add up your score. According to the scale notes, if you score 24 or more then PTSD is a clinical concern. It states that people with scores this high who do not have full PTSD will have partial PTSD or at least some of the symptoms. The notes suggest that a score of 33 or above represents the best cut-off for a probable diagnosis of PTSD. The notes go on to say that a score of 37 indicates a high enough level of stress to suppress your immune system's functioning (even 10 years after an impact event).

The controversies with this test start with the concept of PTSD (see below) which is hard to define and hence even harder to diagnose. The IES-R might well be a reliable test but it reduces complex experience to a series of numbers. And it does this by asking people to answer questions that require them to make comparative judgements about how they believe other people respond in similar circumstances. Tests like this are seductive because they give easy-to-understand data that facilitates research and diagnosis. The controversy is about how tests like this contribute to our narrative of human experience. My view is that they do more harm than good, but I'm in the minority.

Summary

The above brief discussion of the technology of psychological tests gives a flavour of the sophistication of test construction and the practical problems involved in constructing and interpreting tests. The controversies are mainly of a technical nature and concern the potential error in tests and how predictive they can be of future behaviour. The arguments might appear a little remote and technical, but without some understanding of the technicalities it is not possible to argue about the other issues that arise out of psychological testing. We go on now to look at how tests have contributed to our understanding of personality and mental health.

The myth of personality

Personality is a word we use a lot but what does it mean? There is a tension in psychology between capturing the unique experiences of individuals (idio-graphic approach) and looking for the features we share and hence deriving laws

---

1 For example, https://www.aerztenetz-grafschaft.de/download/IES-R-englisch-5-stufig.pdf

of behaviour (nomothetic approach). It is the latter approach that holds sway in psychology and has created a generally held belief that it is possible to categorise and quantify people in order to describe their personality characteristics. This process uses types and traits. Types are categories that we fit people into, and traits are characteristics that people are perceived to vary on. The trait approach is by the far the most common way of researching personality in psychology.

Cattell and Butcher (1968) suggested there are three ways to approach the study of personality:

- The literary approach in which the playwright or novelist describes people in a way that gives the reader an insight into human behaviour and experience.
- Clinical observation in which the clinician attempts to systematically classify normal and abnormal personalities.
- The statistical tradition based on correlational methods and, in particular, factor analysis.

In this section, we will look at this third approach and consider some of the issues around measuring and quantifying personality characteristics. The measurement of personality does not create the same heat of controversy as does the measurement of intelligence (see chapter 5). The main reason for this is that the political impact of personality scores is not as obvious as IQ scores. Many of the same controversial issues, however, can be found in the measurement of both qualities, for example, the use of factor analysis, the validity of the tests, the issues surrounding the inheritance of personal qualities, and the historical connection between psychometric testing and eugenics.

Personality questionnaires

The most popular way of measuring personality is through a questionnaire. The advantages are obvious in that questionnaires are relatively easy to construct, they are relatively easy to use with people, and it is relatively easy to establish norms. In short, they are psychometrically efficient (Kline, 1993). The problems with this approach are first, validity (what do these reliable tests actually measure?), and second, impact (what is the effect of these test on our perceptions of individuals and groups?).

One problem arises with the use of factor analysis. When factor analysis is used to look at intellectual performance there is a theory that predicts how many factors there will be (in this case, one). In personality theory, however, the expected number of factors is by no means so obvious. Nobody would predict that all the differences between individuals can be explained by just one feature of personality, but how many are there? It is possible to come up with a number of factors just by the statistical method of factor analysis. And when you analyse factor analysis data, two different researchers might arrive at a different number of factors from the same data. Even if we get agreement about the number of factors that the data gives us we then have to give these factors a name and show that they really exist.

The alternative explanation is that the factors are just a trick of the numbers and have no existence outside the computer of a statistician.

Theories of personality

In the last half-century, numerous trait personality models have emerged, each claiming to outline the hierarchical structure of human personality. These include the 16-factor model (Cattell, 1957; Cattell, Eber, & Tatsuoka, 1970), the three-factor model (Eysenck & Eysenck, 1991), the five-factor model (McCrae & Costa, 1985) and the six-factor (HEXACO) model (Ashton et al., 2004). There is also an influential alternative three-factor biological personality model the BIS/BAS model (Gray & McNaughton, 2000), which has achieved much popularity in the last few decades.

The five-factor model is arguably the most popular model of personality. It first appeared in 1985 and was developed by McCrae and Costa (1997). The five-factor model is often referred to by its acronym of OCEAN, which stems from the initial letters of the model's five factors: Openness to experience, Conscientiousness, Extraversion, Agreeableness and Neuroticism (Matthews, Deary, & Whiteman, 2003). The personality traits from this model are measured with the self-report NEO Personality Inventory-Revised (NEO PI-R; Costa & McCrae, 1992), although this measure is a lengthy 240-items long. Due to the fatigue that participants get when answering so many questions, researchers more commonly use the shorter 60-item NEO-FFI Questionnaire (Costa & McCrae, 1992).

More recently, still there has been a lot of interest in a further three personality dimensions referred to as the Dark Triad (Paulhus & Williams, 2002). The three characteristics of Machiavellianism, psychopathy and narcissism are argued to describe people who rate high in their willingness to exploit anyone to get ahead, and they experience little remorse when they cause harm to other.[2]

And so it continues, with new formulations of how best to describe people by using a series of tick-box questionnaires and fitting them into a framework with a varying number of dimensions. If we reflect back to the start of this section and ask again what we mean by personality then it is clear there is no general agreement even within the psychometric community on the number of factors that can be used to describe this quality.

Expectation and the Barnum effect

One problem with personality tests comes from the expectations of the people taking the tests. Furnham and Varian (1988) looked at how people predict and accept their own test scores. In their first study, they asked undergraduates to

---

2 If you are interested in this darker side of life, and the darker side of psychometric testing then try reading Jon Ronson's *The Psychopath Test*, which is provocative, interesting and sometimes downright funny.

try and predict their own and a well-known other person's personality scores on a personality test. They were fairly good at this. Then, in a second study, they gave some undergraduates false feedback about their scores after they had completed the test. The undergraduates were more likely to accept positive feedback (e.g., 'you are a warm and considerate person') as accurate than negative feedback (e.g., 'you are miserable and self-centered'), even though it didn't have any connection with their actual scores.

This leads us to an inevitable discussion of the Barnum Effect (so named after the famous American showman, P.T. Barnum). In brief, the Barnum Effect refers to a powerful tendency to believe information given to us about our personal qualities. This can be used to good effect by, for example, fortune tellers, astrologers, and handwriting 'experts'. If the 'expert' can say what people are prepared to accept, and can phrase it in such a way that it implies some intimate insight, then there is a good, if dishonourable living to be made.

An early example of this was provided by Forer (1949) in a classroom demonstration of gullibility. Forer described a personality test to his students and allowed them to persuade him to let them take the test (the first rule of a successful con is to appear reluctant!). Thirty-nine students completed the test. One week later, each was given a typed personality sketch with their name on it. The researcher encouraged the class to keep the results confidential, and the students were asked to indicate whether they thought the test results were accurate. In fact, they had been given identical personality sketches (see Table 4.1) which had no relationship to their test responses, yet all of the students rated the test as a perfect or near-perfect tool for investigating personality. This is a demonstration of the Barnum Effect. If we return to the study by Furnham and Varian (1988), we could argue that this is a demonstration of this same Barnum Effect, and that personality tests are successful, at least in part, because they provide plausible personality sketches. Try it out yourself. Offer to read someone's palm or tea leaves and use the statements on them in a sincere voice. See what their response is.

Problems with personality questionnaires

Kline (1993) identifies a number of sources of error in personality questionnaires including

a   Acquiescence: People have a tendency to agree with items regardless of the content.
b   Social desirability: People prefer to put themselves in a good light and so have a tendency to respond in a way that makes them appear alright. For example, we are unlikely to admit to not washing very often even if that was true.
c   Middle categories: Many questionnaires ask people to respond on a five-point scale, and there is a tendency for people to use the middle value.

Table 4.1 The statements used by Forer (1949) in his demonstration of the Barnum effect

1 You have a great need for other people to like and admire you.
2 You have a tendency to be critical of yourself.
3 You have a great deal of unused capacity which you have not turned to your advantage.
4 5While you have some personality weaknesses, you are generally able to compensate for them.
  Your sexual adjustment has presented problems for you.
6 Disciplined and self-controlled outside, you tend to be worrisome and insecure inside.
7 8At times you have serious doubts as to whether you have made the right decision or done the right thing.
  9You prefer a certain amount of change and variety and become dissatisfied when hemmed in by restrictions and limitations.
  10You pride yourself as an independent thinker and do not accept others' statements without satisfactory proof.
  You have found it unwise to be too frank in revealing yourself to others.
11 12At times you are extroverted, affable, sociable, while at other times you are introverted, wary, reserved.
  Some of your aspirations tend to be pretty unrealistic.
13 Security is one of your major goals in life.

Personality tests are used extensively in occupational and clinical settings. A sophisticated technology has been developed to ensure the reliability of the tests and to produce evidence for their validity. Sometimes, however, the belief in the existence of certain behavioural patterns or personality characteristics can be more powerful than the scientific evidence. For example, the study of coping has been dominated by Folkman and Lazarus (1990) description of coping styles (see Table 4.2). Their eight distinct styles of coping were derived from factor analysis, and their model is extensively applied and researched on. A close look at the data, however, reveals that the eight coping styles are not as distinct as Folkman and Lazarus suggest, and it would be a more accurate reading of the data to talk about only four or five factors (see Ferguson & Cox, 1997). This new analysis has not dented the general belief in the original categories.

Table 4.2 The eight coping strategies identified by Folkman and Lazarus through factor analysis but challenged by Ferguson and Cox

Problem-focused strategies
  1 Confrontive coping
  2 Planful problem solving
Emotion-focused strategies
  1 Distancing
  2 Self-controlling
  3 Seeking social support
  4 Accepting responsibility
  5 Escape-avoidance
  6 Positive reappraisal

Summary

Personality testing is a massive enterprise that attracts a lot of interest from organisations and also the general public. The focus is mainly on tick-box questionnaires that aim to represent the complexity of human experience and behaviour in a small set of numbers. The value of these tests is unknown.

The myth of diagnosis

Paul Lutus writes,

> Like religion, human psychology has a dark secret at its core – it contains within it a model for correct behavior, although that model is never directly acknowledged. Buried within psychology is a nebulous concept that, if it were to be addressed at all, would be called "normal behavior." …
>
> … In the same way that everyone is a sinner in religion's metaphysical playground, everyone is mentally ill in psychology's long, dark hallway – no one is truly "normal." This means everyone needs psychological treatment.
>
> (Lutus, 2020)

Psychological diagnosis has a long history. The Greeks, for example, re-cognised such diagnoses as senility, alcoholism, mania, melancholia and paranoia. The first comprehensive system of psychological disorders[3] was created in 1896 by Emil Kraepelin. He believed that mental disorders have the same basis as physical ones, and that the same diagnostic principles should be applied – the careful observation of symptoms. It is by no means obvious why we should believe that psychological and emotional disturbances have the same bases as say chickenpox or the common cold. However, it is Kraepelin's view (the medical model) that is the dominant one in our modern world.

The myth of mental illness

The medical model was challenged by Thomas Szasz in his paper The Myth of Mental Illness. In his critique, Szasz (1960) argued that the medical model is unhelpful to our understanding of psychiatric conditions. The medical model suggests that all psychiatric problems will eventually be understood in terms of simple chemical reactions and that 'mental illnesses' are basically no different to other diseases. Szasz argued that there are two errors in this view:

---

3 I don't believe that 'disorder' is the best term to use, and I'd prefer to use 'reaction'. The reason for this is that reaction denotes a response to the environment rather than something wrong with the individual. I continue to use 'disorder', however, because that is the term that was used.

First, a disease of the brain is a neurological defect and not a problem of living. For example, a defect in a person's vision may be explained by correlating it with certain lesions in the nervous system. On the other hand, a person's belief, whether this is a belief in Christianity, or Communism, or that they are a robot, cannot be explained by a defect of the nervous system. Some beliefs are perfectly acceptable and some are thought to be a sign of mental disorder, but they are all beliefs.

Second, in medicine when we speak of physical disturbances we mean either signs (e.g., fever) or symptoms (e.g., pain). When we speak about mental symptoms, however, we refer to how patients describe themselves and the world around them. They might say that they are Napoleon or that they are being persecuted by aliens from another planet. These are symptoms only if the observer believes that the patient is not Napoleon, or not being persecuted by aliens. So to see a statement as a mental symptom we have to make a judgement that involves a comparison of the patient's ideas and beliefs with those of the observer and of the society in which they live.

Szasz suggests that the idea of mental illness is being used to obscure the difficulties we have in everyday living. In the Middle Ages, it was witches and devils who were held responsible for the problems in social living. The belief in mental illness is no more sophisticated than a belief in demonology. Mental illness, according to Szasz is 'real' in exactly the same way as witches were 'real'.

Chickenpox and PTSD

When it comes to knowledge in psychology we are not so much uncovering it as inventing it. We appear to use the basic methods of science by observing and categorising behaviour in the much the same way as biologists or medics. But there's a difference, and this difference is nowhere more obvious than in diagnosis. If you compare a medical disorder such as chickenpox with a psychological diagnosis like PTSD then you'll see the contrast.

When we diagnose a physical condition we often look at how someone is differing from what we would normally expect. Maybe their blood pressure is higher than most other people. When we look at a psychological condition then we compare their behaviour or experience not against medical measures such as blood pressure but against what we believe are the social, ethical or legal norms of our society.

To diagnose chickenpox, we look for three symptoms; fever, itchy spots and loss of appetite. That's it. But if we want to diagnose PTSD, we look for any of 19 symptoms arranged in four categories. To make the diagnosis of PTSD, you have to judge the patient to have just eight of these symptoms across the four categories. In other words, two people might each have eight symptoms and achieve a diagnosis of PTSD but not have a single symptom in common. There are, in fact 646,120 ways to get a diagnosis of PTSD (Galatzer-Levy & Bryant, 2013). On top of this, chickenpox has a known pathogen which is a virus. There is no clear pathogen for PTSD. The illness metaphor breaks down on all levels.

PTSD was first described in the third edition of the Diagnostic and Statistical Manual (see below) of the American Psychiatric Association in 1980 in response to the long-term distress shown by many US veterans of the American war in Vietnam. In subsequent revisions, the criteria were expanded and it is now one of the most frequently used diagnosis and has become a catch-all category which pathologises a wide variety of disturbing life events. The dispute is not whether people experience extreme stress reactions to disturbing events (they do) but whether it adds anything to label this and categorise it as an illness.

The Diagnostic and Statistical Manual of Mental Disorders (DSM)

This brings us to a discussion of the DSM.[4] The Diagnostic and Statistical Manual of Mental Disorders, first published in 1952, is the diagnostic bible of US psychiatry and has influenced diagnoses around the world. It is currently in its fifth iteration and is hence known as DSM-5. The DSM structures the way we think about life, behaviour and experience and defines many sorts of behaviour as mental disorders. Over the various versions, disorders have appeared and disappeared. Some of these seem to be matters of politeness and sociability rather than mental health. For example, there is one called Oppositional Defiant Disorder, which you or I might well see as being awkward, and there is Conduct Disorder which might be called naughtiness by someone else.

In the attempt to catalogue mental distress the DSM has turned everyday behaviour into pathological categories and thereby assigned negative labels to ordinary activities. In case you think I am exaggerating the problem, you might consider an article in a prestigious journal that reports that one-third of us have 'excessive anxiety' when asked to speak to large audiences and may be suffering from a mental disorder (Stein, Walker & Forde, 1996). It seems entirely reasonable to be very anxious about speaking in public and especially so to a big audience, and it is difficult to see this anxiety as a sign of a mental disorder. And what about Misophonia? This is a condition observed (created?) to describe the distress felt by some at listening to other people make chewing noises (Schröder et al., 2013).

DSM and homosexuality

The story of how homosexuality has been framed by psychiatry helps us to understand the impact of the DSM. In the first version of the DSM in 1952,

---

4 We are only going to scratch the surface here but if you want to know more about this then pick up Kutchins and Kirk's excellent text, *Making Us Crazy*.

homosexuality was included as a specific diagnosis under the heading 'Sexual Deviation'. It was removed from DSM-3 following protest from gay activists. It was replaced however with a category labelled Ego-Dystonic Homosexuality which was applied to people for whom their sexuality was unwanted and troublesome to them. Given that there were still oppressive anti-gay laws in most countries (including the United Kingdom) at that time it is not surprising that sexuality was troubling for many gay people.

The use of diagnostic categories in this way acts as a control on behaviour and experience, and defines socially acceptable and unacceptable behaviour and lifestyles. It is not helping with experiences of mental distress but instead acting to maintain a status quo that is oppressive and sometimes the source of the stress that a person is experiencing. Another example of this is the way women have had their experience and struggle with misogyny devalued and pathologised with diagnoses such as Self-Defeating Personality Disorder and Masochistic Personality Disorder (Caplan, 1995).

Diagnosis and racism

Science has been the political wing of the war on Black and Brown people waged by White Europeans. One of the battlefields has been mental health. There is a long history of racist psychiatry, and diagnosis has played a central part in adding a scientific gloss to it. For example, a condition was created to describe people in slavery who had an urge to run away from the plantation (drapetomania). Littlewood and Lipsedge (1997) observe that scientific racism peaked under the Nazi governments of Europe in the mid-20th century, though they remind us that:

> … they were only carrying to a logical conclusion racist opinions commonly held throughout Europe and America before the Second World War.
>
> (Littlewood and Lipsedge, 1997, p. 47)

Psychiatry in the United States was segregated in the first half of the 20th century. As late as 1948, the President of the America Psychiatric Association was still opposing desegregation of psychiatric facilities. To do justice to this sorry history would take a whole book and as luck would have it, Littlewood and Lipsedge have written it (see *Aliens and Alienists*).

A quick look at some of the currently available data will illustrate how issues of race are still very much in play in our mental health services. For example, data from the UK government shows that Black people in the United Kingdom are more likely to experience mental distress and are therefore more likely to encounter mental health services. The 2017 Race Disparity Audit found that Black men are ten times more likely than White men to experience a disorder that is categorised as being psychosis (IRR, 2021). And in the year to March 2020, Black people were more than four times as likely as White people to be detained under the Mental Health Act (GOV.UK. 2021). Wherever you look you find the same story of differential diagnosis and differential treatment, and it is always to the detriment of the people from historically marginalised groups.

Reliability and validity of the DSM

Perhaps surprisingly (and perhaps not), there have been relatively few studies looking at the reliability of the DSM as a set of diagnostic criteria. The starting point for these studies is to see whether different psychiatrists will arrive at the same or similar diagnosis when interviewing the same patient. The simple answer is that they don't, leading Kutchins and Kirk to write,

> No study of DSM as a whole in a regular clinical setting has shown uniformly high reliability.
>
> (Kutchins & Kirk, 1997, p. 50)

The criticisms don't just come from people opposed to diagnosis per se. Allen Frances once chaired the committee working on the development of the DSM. He wrote of the latest version,

> There is no reason to believe that DSM-5 is safe or scientifically sound.
>
> (Frances, 2013)

> *DSM-5* hoped to include biological markers that might reflect past research and promote future research. This was a premature and unrealisable ambition: the science simply isn't there now. And it has become increasingly clear that the *DSM* descriptive system may be a research dead end because its syndromes are too diverse and overlapping to be good research targets (ibid).

The conclusion I draw about the DSM is that it functions as a tool to maintain the status quo and to defend the interests of powerful groups at the expense of the powerless. It is neither reliable nor valid and yet it still has so much support. I think this support is fueled by a belief in the value of the categorisation process and a belief in medical explanations of human distress, both of which I suggest are false beliefs.

Consequences of diagnosis

One of the factors that keep diagnosis central to our response to mental distress is that a diagnosis will give you access to treatment and resources including insurance claims. A diagnosis then can be very useful and so we are locked into this negative and unreliable analysis of mental health. One of the consequences of this is that the first stop for any treatment is still based on a medical model and commonly involves physical treatments such as medication. For example, in the United Kingdom, there has been an inexorable rise in the number of prescriptions for anti-depressants for the last 30 years. By 2020, the number of prescriptions had exceeded 80 million per year (Robinson, 2021). In a country of just 70 million people, that's an awful lot of happy pills. The level of distress still experienced in this country is testimony to the effectiveness (not) of these medications.

Diagnosis is the gateway to treatment and the default treatments are medications. It is no surprise then to find out that the major sponsors of the DSM and its development are the international pharmaceutical companies (often referred to as Big Pharma) who provide these medications.

Is it mad to be happy?

On a lighter note and in a gentle parody of psychiatric diagnosis, Richard Bentall (1992) proposed that happiness should be classed as a mental disorder and referred to under the new name of *major affective disorder, pleasant type*. In his article, he suggested that the relevant literature shows that happiness is statistically abnormal, is made up of a discrete cluster of symptoms, is associated with a range of cognitive abnormalities, and probably reflects the abnormal functioning of the central nervous system. He considered the possible objection that happiness is not thought badly of but he dismissed it as scientifically irrelevant. You would think that an article like this would contribute the sum of human happiness but sadly some people took it seriously and it made them sad. Humour is a serious business.

Alternatives to diagnosis

Psychiatric diagnosis has been with us for over 100 years and is still going strong despite all the evidence that challenges its reliability, validity and usefulness. But if this chapter seems like a treaty of despair, there is some hope to be had in the work of clinical psychologists in the United Kingdom. The Division of Clinical Psychology (in the British Psychological Society) issued an official statement calling for the end of psychiatric diagnosis and the medical model of mental distress (BPS, 2013). Getting a statement like this from a professional organisation is no mean feat and signals a change in the way that mental distress is being seen in the United Kingdom.

One of the key advocates of this approach is Lucy Johnstone (see, e.g., Johnstone, 2014, 2018). She proposes using formulation rather than diagnosis. In essence, instead of asking 'what is wrong with you?' (diagnosis), you ask 'what has happened to you?'. In this approach, you build up a picture of the events and experiences that led up to the current situation where the person is seeking support for their distress. If this approach is followed then a diagnosis (in which the experience is labelled and categorised) is irrelevant.

There is also a large and influential movement of former psychiatric patients who are unhappy with the treatment they received in psychiatry and are campaigning for alternatives that are not based on a medical model. One of the best known is the *Hearing Voices Network* (www.intervoice.org) which has enabled many people to reject their diagnoses and find ways of living happily with their voices. An eloquent example is Eleanor Longden, who can be heard telling her story at a TED talk (Longden, 2013). She was labelled as schizo-phrenic and told she was a hopeless case until she met a psychiatrist who helped her to recover from the traumas of her childhood.

Summary

Categorising people by their abilities or their experiences is a prominent feature of how psychology behaves in Western societies in the 21st century. The categorisation process is flawed. With regard to diagnoses, we are not discovering disorders, we are inventing them. This process of invention can pathologise everyday life and create more problems for people than it can ever hope to solve. But, don't take my word for this, check out some of the readings I have suggested in the chapter.

5   Mental testing

The testing of intelligence is perhaps the most longstanding controversy in psychology. The following two quotes give some idea of the spread of opinion on this topic.

> The measurement of intelligence is psychology's most telling accomplishment to date.
>
> (Herrnstein, 1971, p. 45)

> There exist no data which should lead a prudent *[person]* to accept the hypotheses that IQ test scores are in any degree heritable ... the IQ test has served as an instrument of oppression against the poor.
>
> (Kamin, 1977, pp. 1–2)

In the spirit of full disclosure, I stand with Kamin on this. The concept of intelligence is a further example of psychology's almost pathological need to quantify human experience and to create categories to put people into. This chapter develops some of the points from the previous one on categories and also the one before that on racism in psychology.

The creation of the intelligence myth

The word intelligence has its root in Greek and the idea has a long history though it has been thought of in different ways over time (Goodey, 2011). Our modern understanding of the term in the UK, however, is not much more than 100 years old and arrived with the introduction of mass schooling for children and a perceived need to rank them in order of their abilities. This attempt to rank people was controversial when it was introduced and remains controversial today, and part of that controversy comes from the common understanding of the term – that intelligence is something we are probably born with. When we rank people by their intelligence, are we ranking their natural talent or their schooling and social environment? Whichever answer we choose has big implications for how we should organise our education

DOI: 10.4324/9781003147589-5

system and how we should treat children who do not do well on the tests of intelligence.

The first mental tests

The earliest psychometric testing is usually attributed to Francis Galton who set up a stall at the International Health Exhibition in London in 1884 and tested visitors' mental abilities for the sum of 3 pence. As many as 9,000 people took the tests which included measures of reaction times to sounds, lights and touch, and other easily measurable motor activities and sensory judgements. As we saw in chapter 3, Galton had an agenda and he hoped to use these measures to estimate people's hereditary intelligence. Before Galton, psychology had been looking for general principles of experience. By contrast, Galton's anthropometric laboratory looked to quantify and categorise people, and so the field of individual differences was born. Although we would not recognise Galton's tests and measures of mental abilities, today they do mark the beginning of mental testing.

The first tests of intelligence were developed in France by Alfred Binet (1857–1911) who started his scientific studies by examining the relationship between head size and intelligence. Although you might expect that *big head = big brain = big intelligence,* Binet discovered that there is no relationship between these factors.

In France, at that time, the government had just introduced universal basic education for children. Problems emerged with children who couldn't keep up and, in particular, some children who appeared so weak at school that it appeared that they might not benefit from this type of education at all. Binet, along Théodore Simon, a young paediatrician, devised tests to identify slow learners. In 1904, the French government set up a commission that included both Simon and Binet to examine this question. The following year the two scientists published their first test aimed at distinguishing children with learning difficulties.

In its original form (in 1905), the Binet-Simon test had 30 sub-tests ranging in difficulty from simple eye movements to definitions of abstract concepts. The sub-tests were arranged in order of difficulty so that the further a child got in the test the more developed their intelligence was assumed to be. In the 1908 version of the test, Binet and Simon went beyond just identifying the slow learners and started to distinguish different levels of performance in all children. The tests were given to lots of children and average performance was calculated for each age of the child. This allowed them to say how any child compared to the other children and therefore they could say that Boris, for example, was performing at the level of the average four-year-old even though he was 57.

The creation of the intelligence quotient (IQ)

Binet's view was that intelligence was a collection of factors rather than a single one. He was not a supporter of the inheritance view of intelligence, and although he believed that genetics puts limits on development, he thought that there is a big part to be played by the environment and education. He was also very cautious about labelling children and he warned that even when children performed at two or three years below their chronological age it did not mean that they had mental disabilities. In fact, it was Binet's view that disadvantaged children could be prepared for school with mental exercises (Hergenhahn, 2001).

In 1911, German psychologist William Stern suggested the term *mental age* to describe the performance on the Binet-Simon tests compared to the average performance. So, if an individual child obtained the same score as the average for a 6-year-old, then they were said to have a mental age of 6. Stern went further to suggest that this could be represented as a ratio with their chronological age as shown below and the concept of the Intelligence Quotient (IQ was born).[1]

$$\text{Intelligence Quotient (IQ)} = \text{Mental Age}/\text{Chronological Age} \times 100$$

Using this formula, if an 8-year-old child has a mental age of 8 (the average) their IQ will be $8/8 \times 100 = 100$. And if they have a mental age of 10 their IQ will be $8/10 \times 100 = 125$.

Binet did not approve of reducing intelligence to a single number, but it was Stern's view that prevailed and it is how we view the concept today. After Stern, the calculation of IQ has become more sophisticated. It is now based on *norm referencing*, or in other words, it depends on calculating the average performance for your peers then comparing you against the average.

The creation of g (the general factor of intelligence)

Something quite dramatic has happened here. Binet and Simon devised some tests to look at a range of cognitive abilities and this has now been condensed into a single number. The numbers have now created a new concept, that of a single underlying cognitive quality that describes a person's overall ability and performance on a wide range of activities. This concept was not driven by theory or evidence, just by expediency (the availability of a number) and a belief by some scientists in the validity of quantifying and categorizing people. And, as already mentioned, those scientists had an agenda about quantifying people and promoting white supremacy.

Charles Spearman was impressed by the attempts of Galton to measure mental abilities and started to devise his own tests. He was also in agreement with Galton about the inheritance of intelligence and the value of eugenics. His tests were not very successful but his work on how to analyse the data led to the development of *factor analysis* for which he is still remembered today.

Spearman observed that people who were good on one feature of the

---

1 The idea to multiply the ratio by 100 was added by Terman a few years later.

intelligence test such as maths problems also tended to do well on other features such as vocabulary. He suggested that these correlations indicated that there was an underlying factor that influence all these scores. He called this factor *general intelligence* which is commonly abbreviated to *g*. He further proposed that each individual test measured a *specific intelligence* (abbreviated to *s*) and so the theory is often referred to a two-factor theory of intelligence.

Spearman needed to find a way of showing that g was an underlying factor in these correlations and so he devised factor analysis. This is a complex statistical procedure that examines all the inter-correlations of many factors and draws out patterns of relatedness. Spearman's creation of factor analysis provided mathematical support for his idea about *g*. The skeptical might wonder whether there is a connection between these two things. If you look hard enough for something you will always find[2] it and the initial evidence for g was provided by someone who was committed to the idea using a mathematical procedure that few people understood.

One intelligence or many?

One of the key battlegrounds for intelligence is whether there is one underlying characteristic that we can call intelligence or whether there is a range of independent skills and abilities. Our everyday understanding is that we can use the term to describe a very wide range of activities which implies there is an underlying characteristic that drives them all. As we have already noted, in psychology this characteristic is usually referred to as '*g*' (the general factor of intelligence) but the argument rages around whether it even exists.

One of the arguments against *g* is that we have evidence of very specific intelligences, for example, musical intelligence. Some people can develop advanced musical intelligence if it is adaptive in their community. Lord (1960) studied how singers of oral verse in a rural Balkan community became singers of epic songs. This requires a high level of linguistic and musical intelligence because the singer has to learn musical and linguistic formulae that allow them to construct appropriate songs. This is no mean feat as each song lasts throughout a whole evening, and a different song is sung on each of the forty days of the holy month of Ramadan. The singer has to learn the skill by observation of these events for many years, practice in private and then perform in front of a critical audience.

Another example can be seen in navigational intelligence. Many of us are capable of getting lost in Sainsbury's so the idea that some people can navigate across thousands of miles is almost unimaginable. This is an essential skill, however, in island communities such as Micronesia where islands can be

---

2 The exception to this is when you have lost your nephew's Lego batman Minifigure which will remain lost until you have bought a new one, at which point it will magically re-materialise under the settee.

thousands of miles apart. Gladwin (1970) studied how men in the Puluwat Islands of Micronesia train to become master navigators. This position is achieved by very few individuals because it demands an extremely high aptitude, involving a combination of different kinds of intelligence. The master navigators must memorise vast amounts of factual information such as the identities and locations of all the islands to which anyone might travel to, the names and paths of all of the stars which a navigator can use to spot their course, and the techniques for using this information to devise a route. They also have to develop exceptional practical skills involved with sea travel such as reading currents, the weather and the waves.

Despite the evidence of the special intelligences, the general factor (g) still retains a lot of support though reviews have found over 70 different abilities that can be distinguished by mental testing (Carroll, 1993). One of the key supporters of g was Arthur Jensen who became a controversial figure because of his writings about racial differences in intelligence. These observations lead to our final point about intelligence in this section and that refers to why it matters.

While you have been reading this you might wonder why it matters if there is one intelligence (g) or many intelligences or even no intelligence at all. The simple answer is that it matters because the answer to this question has the power to affect people's lives. If there is no g, then this means that we each have a unique profile of intelligent skills but no overall level of intelligence, so there is no point ranking us, and no point in having an IQ score. Furthermore, if you take the issue of the inheritance of individual differences in intelligence, then if there is no such thing as a general factor of intelligence then it is difficult to argue that this non-existent thing is under genetic control. However, if there is a g and if the differences between people are under genetic control then certain implications follow. For example, it implies that it is not possible to do anything about children who do not do well on IQ tests and the best thing to do would be to concentrate our resources on those who getter higher scores on IQ tests. More frighteningly, we might argue that the way they improve the general intelligence of the nation would be to encourage people with high intelligence to have more children and those with low intelligence to have less. And this brings us back once more to eugenics.

Suddenly, the story of intelligence stops being an abstract academic debate and starts being about how we want to live and how we want to run our society. We'll explore this later, but for now, we go back to the story of how the concept of intelligence developed and was used.

Summary

The concept of intelligence is relatively modern and was created and supported by people with a political agenda that involved the promotion of selective breeding (eugenics) and the belief in white supremacy. The concept requires the existence of an underlying factor that affects most cognitive functions. The factor (g) is essential to the argument but has minimal evidence to support its existence. And so the myth of intelligence was created.

Mass testing

The move to the United States

The next big development in this story took place in the United States. The Binet-Simon test was translated into English by Henry Goddard and then amended by Lewis Terman who named his version the *Stanford-Binet Test* (after the university where he was professor of psychology). Between them, they developed and popularised the tests in the United States to the point that during the 1920s 4 million were sold each year (Schultz, 1996). Both Terman and Goddard were committed to the belief that differences between people in their intelligence were the result of genetic differences and were therefore under hereditary control. Both men developed research to support this view and we will examine the controversial consequences of this later.

Within ten years of Binet's death, the view that he held of intelligence had been effectively usurped by people using the tests that he developed. The common view of intelligence that emerged was of a single factor (*g*) that could be reduced to a single number (IQ) and was the product of heredity. In contrast to the approach of Binet, the fiercest supporters of intelligence testing in the English speaking world were scientists who believed that individual differences are mainly due to genetic factors, and who proposed eugenic solutions to the perceived problems of society. For example, Lewis Terman wrote,

> If we would preserve our state for a class of people worthy to possess it, we must prevent, as far as possible, the propagation of mental degenerates
> (Lewis Terman, 1921, cited in Kamin, 1977)

The big words disguise the sentiments of the quote. To paraphrase Terman, he is saying we must stop poor and uneducated people from having children. We will see the consequences of this belief below.

The first mass IQ testing

American psychologist Robert Yerkes was concerned to establish psychology as a 'hard' science and thought that mental testing looked like a promising route to achieve this. Unfortunately, in 1915 mental testing did not enjoy much credibility, so Yerkes tried to change this. The outbreak of The Great War (1914–1918) in Europe and the subsequent involvement of the United States brought about a massive mobilisation of armies. Yerkes managed to persuade the American military to give mental tests to all army recruits, and as a result he was able to preside over the testing of 1.75 million recruits.

There were three types of tests: literate recruits were given a written test called the Army Alpha, men who were illiterate or who failed the Alpha were given a pictorial test called the Army Beta, and failures on the Beta were to be

Part six of examination Beta for testing innate intelligence

Figure 5.1 Some items from the pictorial part of Yerkes mental tests.

Source: From Yerkes, R.M. (ed) 1921. Psychological examining in the United States army. Memoirs of the National Academy of Sciences, vol 15.

recalled for an individual spoken examination. The Alpha had eight parts made up of the items we recognise today as IQ tests such as analogies, filling in the missing number and unscrambling a sentence. The Beta test had seven parts including number work and the picture completion task shown in Figure 5.1. Each test took less than an hour and could be administered to large groups.

Yerkes was sure that the tests measured 'native intellectual ability' (cited in Gould, p. 349), in other words, intelligence that was unaffected by culture and educational opportunities. He was in the same camp as Terman and Goddard here. The problem with this position, however, can be seen in the level of cultural and educational knowledge required to do the tests and this is clearly illustrated in the examples given below:

> Example 1: Washington is to Adams as first is to ....
> Example 2: Crisco is a: patent medicine, disinfectant, toothpaste, food product.
> Example 3: Christy Mathewson is famous as a: writer, artist, baseball player, comedian.

You might be able to see how the first item works; Washington was the first President of the United States and so the missing word refers to where in the line of Presidents Adams came. Unless you are good on the history of the United States you have no chance. Likewise, with the second item, you need to be familiar with the inside of a US grocery store to answer that one and for the third item, you need to be a sports fan (the answer is baseball player).

There were a number of problems in the administration of the tests. In particular, many of the service people who were illiterate in English were still allocated to the Alpha test and so scored zero or near to zero. Yerkes had overestimated the level of literacy in the general population and so the queues for the Beta tests became very long, leading to the inappropriate reallocation of men to the Alpha test. Failures on the Alpha test were often not recalled to take the Beta test. This created a systematic bias in the test since recent immigrants who had a poor grasp of English, and Black soldiers who had not been given much, if any, formal education, were unable to score on the Alpha test. Another problem was that even the Beta test required the use of a pencil and the writing of numbers, and many men had never held a pencil in their lives. Gould outlines a number of other problems with the testing procedures which suggest that the data should be looked at with considerable scepticism. However, at the time, the results had a considerable impact, and by the end of the war, some of the army camps were using the tests to screen people for officer training.

The tests generated a lot of interest, and by 1921, when Yerkes published his findings, he was able to refer to 'the steady stream of requests from commercial concerns, educational institutions and individuals for the use of army methods of psychological examining or for adaptation of such methods to special needs' (cited in Gould, p. 351). Mental testing and psychology had achieved the credibility that Yerkes wanted.

The misuse of the data

Stephen Jay Gould (1982, 1996) in his excellent account of the testing suggests that three key 'facts'[3] were created at this time:

---

3 When he refers to 'facts', Gould means that three widely held beliefs were created by the data and many people came to see them as accurate statements of truth (facts) rather than partial interpretations of the evidence (opinion). We would refer to this as fake news today.

i   'The average mental age of White US adults stood just above the edge of moronity at a shockingly meagre 13. Terman had previously set the standard at 16' (Gould, 1982, p. 351).
ii   It was possible to grade European immigrants by their country of origin. According to the test results, the average man of many countries was a moron, with the fair people of Northern and Western Europe scoring higher than the Slavs of Eastern Europe and the people of Southern Europe.
iii The average score of Black men was 10.4, which was considerably below the White average.

Although the 'finding' that the average US citizen was a moron caused some concern, this was nothing compared to the response to the other two 'facts'. These were used to support the idea of genetic differences between races. Carl Brigham, one of Yerkes' colleagues, argued for a genetic explanation of data and proposed the racial superiority of Nordic people (from Northern Europe).

This line of argument was threatened by two problems with the data. First, the immigration of different national groups had taken place at different times, and the most recent immigrants, and hence the least familiar with English, were the Slavs and the people from Southern Europe. So if literacy was having an effect on the test scores, then these people would be disadvantaged. Second, the data showed that the average score rose with the length of residence in the United States. This is a clear indication that the more experience a person had of the United States the higher their score was on the test, suggesting a cultural bias in the questions. Brigham, however, argued quite bizarrely that these data showed that the early immigrants were the brightest from each national group, and the subsequent immigrants were progressively more stupid. He later re-canted this view but not before the damage had been done.

Scientific racism

So, despite the evidence, the racist argument took hold and one of the consequences of this was the passing of the Immigration Restriction Act in 1924 by the US Congress. The scientists who supported this argument lobbied the politicians and, according to Gould, 'won one of the greatest victories of scientific racism in American history' (Gould 1982, p. 352). The Act set immigration quotas based on the US population in 1890 (over 30 years prior to the Act). This year was used as the benchmark because immigration from Southern and Eastern Europe had been relatively low before this date.

During the next 20 years, conditions deteriorated dramatically in Europe for Slavs and Jews as the Nazi governments followed the eugenic ideas and enacted policies of 'racial purity' culminating in genocide. Gould tells how many people tried to flee the political oppression but were denied access to the United States. Estimates suggest that the immigration quotas barred up to six million people from Southern, Central and Eastern Europe, a number with some significance in the history of Europe.

The impact of mass testing

The results of the mass testing were falsely interpreted to give support to the idea that differences in intelligence have a genetic basis. A closer look at the data however reveals that it doesn't really tell us anything about the reason for differences in groups scores, only that the differences in IQ performance exist. However, that is not how it was read at the time.

Galton, along with the other eugenicists, had noticed that better health care and social conditions meant that not so many people were dying at a young age and their reaction to this was a fear that the effect of natural selection was being blunted. In other words, if the weak survive then they will pass on their weak genes to the next generation, They proposed that instead of allowing the environment to selectively breed the better members of the species, this selection should be taken on by people. This selective breeding of a superior class of people could then be used to 'improve society' and ensure the position and influence of people like themselves or in other words the continuance of White supremacy.

These ideas were enthusiastically embraced in the United States where there were concerns about the possible decline of the genetic stock of the nation. Terman and Goddard who brought IQ testing to the United States were supporters of this view as was Spearmen in the UK. These concerns were fuelled by evidence from Yerkes' mass testing which was used as justification for mass sterilisation programmes. The argument here, as mentioned above, was that if differences in intelligence are inherited then we can improve the average intelligence of the nation by stopping people with low intelligence from having children.

Although this seems barely credible, in the United States between 1927 and 1957 it is estimated that approximately 60,000 people labelled either feebleminded or insane underwent sterilisation at state institutions in the name of building a better society (Stubblefield, 2007). The aim of this programme was to eliminate the opportunities for these people to have children and therefore reduce and maybe eliminate learning disabilities from the population. These sterilisations were often carried out without the person knowing, at a time when they were in the hospital for another reason such as giving birth (Park and Radford, 1998). Elsewhere the procedure continued as late as 1976 in Sweden (Denekens et al., 1999). In Germany by 1937, an estimated 225,000 people with mental illness or learning disability had been sterilised (Spann, 1975).

Scientific sexism

As we saw above and in Chapter 3, science has been used to justify a number of racist beliefs. It has also been used to justify a number of sexist ones. There was a prevailing belief in 19th-century science that women were inferior to men. For example, Darwin wrote,

The chief distinction in the intellectual powers of the two sexes is shown by man's attaining to a higher eminence, in whatever he takes up, than can woman – whether requiring deep thought, reason, or imagination, or merely the use of the senses and hands.

(Darwin, cited in Shields, 1978, p. 752)

One of the 'findings' of this period came from the pioneering physiological psychologist, Broca who studied the relative sizes of people's brains. He concluded that on average, women have smaller brains than men and that this meant they were less intelligent than men. As Gould (1978) pointed out, however, the averages were not adjusted to take account of height (taller people have bigger brains), or age (older people are more likely to have reduced brain size). The women in Broca's sample were smaller and older than the men, and these factors explain the difference in the average size of the brains studied by Broca.

Summary

Mental testing became psychology's big idea and a belief developed in the value and efficacy of IQ tests in particular. The main supporters of this approach had a social agenda that supported eugenic arguments and practices and was also openly racist. The consequences of this approach are still being felt today.

The Bell Curve

You might have built up an impression that much of this argument is historical but you would be wrong. The controversy reappears regularly because it is on the fault lines of academic thought and social concerns, and those fault lines are around class and race, power and privilege. It all gets dressed up in flimsy scientific clothes but it is the same arguments that Galton and the other eugenicists put forward.

The normal distribution

Before we continue with the story of intelligence we are going to have a short interlude to look at some statistical ideas (stay with me here).

The normal distribution is a mathematical function that is represented in Figure 5.2. It is often called the Bell Curve for obvious reasons and we'll come back to that later. This mathematical function creates a curve that matches the observations we make in the real world. For example, if we measure the foot size of the population we will find that a large number of people have similar sizes and that a few people have either very large or very small feet. If we plot that distribution on a chart with shoe size on the x-axis (along the bottom) and number of people with this shoe size on the y-axis (up the side), we will get a line very close to a normal distribution. This is very useful information for Skechers, for example, so that they stock the right number of each size of shoe in their shops (other makes of shoe are available).

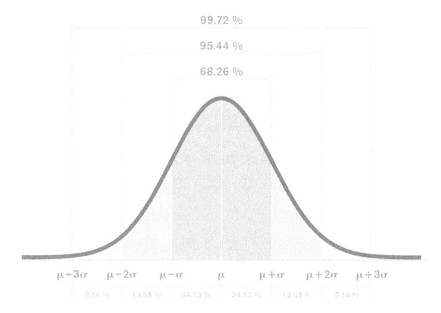

Figure 5.2 The normal distribution.

One of the interesting things about the normal distribution is that because it is a mathematical equation we can do various manipulations with it and find out the characteristics of the sample we are looking at. For example, we can calculate the standard deviation (which is how spread out the scores are) and once we know that we can say where any individual is placed in the whole population. We know that 68.2% of all scores (two-thirds to you and me) are within one standard deviation of the mean score and that over 95% of all scores are within two standard deviations of the mean. I know you are probably glazing over but stay with this for just a bit more.

With regard to IQ scores, the mean score is 100 (by definition, see above) and the tests are designed so that the standard deviation is 15 IQ points. This means that 68% of the population score between 85 and 115 on their IQ test. This is not very much variation and unless IQ tests are very accurate (with little or no tolerance in the values they give) then it suggests that most people have almost indistinguishable levels of IQ. Using the normal distribution, we can take an individual's IQ score and say where they are placed in the rank order of the population. So if you score 100, then you achieved the average score and you are halfway up the rank. If you scored 115, then you are a bit further up the rank and we know that only 13.6% of the population scored any better. And if you scored 130 (2 standard deviations above the mean) then we know that only 2% of the population scored more. This means that if we accept that IQ tests are measuring a general cognitive ability then we can identify people who are intellectually gifted by selecting those that score over 130 on an IQ test.

So why is the normal distribution important and why does it appear in this book on controversies? The issue concerns the heritability of intelligence. If intelligence is affected by a number of clever genes (made up term), then you would expect most people to have some of the clever genes and a few people to have either a lot of or very few of these clever genes, and the expression of this quality would appear in the population in much the same way as foot size does. You would expect a normal distribution of IQ scores, and this is what we get. However, IQ tests are specifically designed to get this distribution and so is not the same as the observations we make about shoe size. But, by talking about intelligence in these terms we are giving manufactured support to a genetic explanation of intelligence. There are also issues about how we interpret these data but this statistical interlude has been long enough.

The book

In 1994, the controversy about IQ was re-ignited by the publication of *The Bell Curve* written by Richard Herrnstein and Charles Murray which set out to explain the variations in intelligence in the United States. The basic premise of *The Bell Curve* is that intelligence is one of the most (if not THE most) important characteristics in a person's life. It will predict their successes and failures much better than any other factor including their socio-economic status. The book is built on six key assumptions about cognitive tests such as IQ:

1   There is a general factor of intelligence and people vary in their abilities.
2   Most mental tests measure this factor to some extent though it is best measured by IQ tests.
3   IQ scores are a good measure of intelligence.
4   IQ scores are relatively stable during a person's life (in other words, individuals don't appear to be able to improve).
5   IQ tests are culture-free and do not favour any groups of people.
6   Differences in cognitive ability are partly inherited, and the amount of the difference that is due to genetic factors is between 40% and 80%.

From what you have already read in this chapter which disputes all of these assertions, you can see that the book was going to attract controversy from page one, and that was the case. The book did indeed create a storm with a lot of people challenging the ideas but also a lot of people supporting them.

In the first part of the book, Herrnstein and Murray argue that the United States is becoming stratified by intelligence. In other words, an upper class is developing because of clever people and the poor people are poor because they are stupid. A more plausible analysis (and one that has some evidence to support it) is that the United States, and in fact the UK, is stratified on the basis of wealth. People with economic power get the best education, the best jobs and the best health care[4]. They live longer, earn more and are more likely to achieve positions of power. By contrast, Herrnstein and Murray are arguing that class and wealth and not important in the United States and certainly not in comparison to intelligence. They go on to argue that the United States is segregating itself on the basis of intelligence and the implication of this is that the cognitive divide (if it exists) is growing.

In the second part of their book Herrnstein and Murray examine evidence that connects social problems with IQ. The overall picture they draw is of IQ being the main predictor of good social adjustment. They argue that low IQ is associated with poverty, dropping out of school, low achievement in school, unemployment, high divorce rates, welfare dependency and criminal behaviour. An alternative reading of the relationship might see the first item in the list – poverty – as the key variable that the others flow from. In fact, research in the UK has found that poverty is a key factor in school performance and how children are treated within the school (Fisher Family Trust, 2011). This is one of the battle lines for the controversy.

Herrnstein and Murray go on to present evidence that low IQ also correlates with issues to do with parenting such as low birth weight for baby, the poor development of motor skills, the poor development of social skills in the child and also the child's chances of showing difficult behaviours from the age of 4. Add to this a further observation that people with low IQ are less likely to vote or to care much about political issues and you have a very negative picture of these people.

The third part of the book looks at differences between groups of people especially groups of people from different ethnic backgrounds. Herrnstein and Murray marshal their evidence to return to arguments made by Galton and later Terman that support ideas of White supremacy. They also revisit the eugenic argument that the average IQ of the United States is likely to go down because the people with low IQ have more children and have them younger than people with high IQ.

Finally, they make some suggestions about changes in social policy that would deal with the conclusions they draw. These include such things as encouraging adoption of children from low IQ mothers, focusing education on gifted rather than below-average children and restricting affirmative action programmes so that they only give advantage to people from disadvantaged groups when qualification levels are the same as other candidates.

Response to the book

The striking thing about the response was the level of support it attracted. Given the nature of the evidence and toxicity of the basic assumptions, you

4 In the history of the UK Parliament, we have had just 55 Prime Ministers of which 20 were educated at Eaton. Either we believe that the brightest and the best go to Eaton (seems unlikely, I've met some of them, Ed.) or that influence in the UK is controlled by a wealthy and powerful elite.

would think that the book would be largely ignored or universally trashed. It was revisiting theoretical ideas with minimal support and rehashing racist and class-based arguments that had been refuted years before. Sadly, many were prepared to rally to this confederate flag.

There was a sustained and detailed challenge to the evidence and conclusions of *The Bell Curve* by leaders in their fields such as Stephen Jay Gould (see above) Howard Gardener (also see above) and Leon Kamin (see his text on the topic). Their arguments pick apart the data and come to different conclusions about what it means. Not everyone was hostile to the book, however, and it is possible to see the argument dividing along political lines with the broad left largely opposed to it and right supporting it. To check out the responses, go to any of the many internet pages that look at this debate.

The arguments against the general position of the book have mainly been dealt with earlier in the chapter, but we will look at how the argument developed. The difficulty for the reader is to try and separate the science from the politics, if this is indeed either possible or desirable.

The evidence

The evidence around the claims of *The Bell Curve* is mixed, but the first thing to establish is that it is all collected and analysed within the framework of Western science using methods and analytical techniques that were developed to further a political agenda (see above and also chapter 3). These methods and techniques stack the deck towards the eugenicist and racist arguments. Having said that, the detailed reviews of the evidence do not provide much, if any, support for the assertions of *The Bell Curve*.

Following the publication of *The Bell Curve*, the American Psychological Association (APA) came to the conclusion that there was a need for an authoritative report on intelligence and 'one that all sides could use as a basis for discussion' (Neisser, 1996, p. 77). A task force was created which was chaired by the highly esteemed Ulrich Neisser and included ten other academics with a broad range of expertise and opinions including some supporters of the ideas in the book.

The report was published by the APA in 1995 and an edited version appeared in the *American Psychologist* the following year (Neisser, 1996). The extensive and very detailed report was unanimously endorsed by all of the task force which is a testament to the consensus making skills of Neisser and also the professionalism of the task force members. As you can see from our earlier description of the controversies, consensus between the different camps is very hard to achieve. The report gives a measured, detailed and dispassionate account of the evidence on intelligence. It does not fall into either of the entrenched political positions and provides support and challenge to both sets of arguments. As a contribution to scientific debate it is a measured and thoughtful document, and if you are interested then look it up on the internet. It does not, however, challenge the scientific context of the research into intelligence which I argue is inherently racist.

Summary

The views and programme for social change (eugenics) proposed by Galton has not gone away despite being soundly discredited by science and history. On a regular cycle, the views are recycled and the argument has to be had again. Keep your eyes out for the next version of this, it won't be long in coming.

The continuing obsession with intelligence and IQ testing

This chapter started with a section on the myth of intelligence. I hope that I have successfully argued that it is a socially constructed idea that is part of an attempt to categorise and rank human beings on their perceived differences in activities and abilities that are judged to be important. From my standpoint, the evidence is clear that although we can identify a range of skills that people display there is little or no evidence of an underlying skill that affects all of the individual ones. In other words, intelligence, as presented to us, does not exist in any definable or measurable form.

Given the above, the continuing use of IQ tests is even more remarkable. Along with the objections I have already raised, there are numerous examples of how they don't match everyday displays of intelligent behaviour. One example is shown by a study of expertise in betting on horse races which found that the reasoning of the most skilled people was implicitly based on a complex mental model with as many as seven variables. However, the level of performance of individuals at gambling did not correlate with their IQ scores (Ceci & Liker, 1986). Similarly, Brazilian street children have been shown to be quite capable of doing the maths required for survival in their street business even though they have failed mathematics in school (Carraher, Carraber, & Schliemann, 1985).

Intelligence boosting

So powerful is the myth of intelligence that multi-million-pound businesses have developed to sell products that are claimed to improve intelligence. One example of the public appetite for intelligence boosting is the Mozart Effect. This effect allegedly shows the cognitive benefits of listening to the music of Mozart. Studies by Rauscher, Shaw, and Ky (1993) examined the effect of listening to the first 10 minutes of the Mozart Sonata for Two Pianos in D Major. They reported a temporary improvement in visual-spatial reasoning on the Stanford-Binet test. Perhaps not surprisingly, replication of this finding has been very difficult outside of their laboratory (Steele, Bass, & Crook, 1999). This lack of scientific support has not dented interest in this idea and an industry has developed around the Mozart effect. You can see it for yourself at their website (http://www.mozarteffect.com) where you can still purchase all manner of products to boost the intelligence of your child. Before you sign up to purchase though you might like to know that much of Mozart's music is available on budget CDs and downloads.

The true description of the Mozart Effect concerns not the impact of music on intelligence but the enduring gullibility of people for snake oil remedies. When we want something very much then we are vulnerable to the false claims of pseudoscience. So the Mozart Effect is best described as the willingness of otherwise intelligent people to spend money on worthless products in the mistaken belief that it will make their children more intelligent.

Smart drugs

Another area that shows the appetite for intelligence boosting products is smart drugs. There is an increasing trend for healthy people, especially students, to take drugs that they believe will enhance their decision-making and general cognitive abilities (Sahakian & Morein-Zamir, 2007). They are not being prescribed for this use but are commonly obtained either for another therapeutic purpose or through internet purchase. Some of the drugs are designed for people with conditions such as Alzheimer's disease, Parkinson's disease and Attention Deficit and Hyperactivity Disorder (ADHD). Their impact and long-term effect on healthy people has not been fully tested.

One of the common drugs used for the purpose of boosting cognitive performance is Ritalin which is prescribed for people with ADHD. The Care Quality Commission has recorded a 50% increase in prescription for drugs like this in the five years up to 2012 (Donnelly, 2013). There is evidence that small gains are observed in attention, working memory and decision-making have been found in healthy adults taking these stimulant drugs (Greely et al., 2008), so maybe this is something that will grow in popularity. Of course, students might take the radical route of deciding to study hard and avoid the need for 'brain boosting' drugs.

Summary

The psychological study of intelligence has a long and controversial history. There is general belief (not shared by the author) that it is possible to accurately measure cognitive abilities and to put people in rank order. There is also a general consensus (also not shared by the author) that this ranking process is a good thing. There are disagreements about the causes of these differences and what interventions we should make to respond to them. The answers you come to will depend less on your reading of the scientific evidence and more on your view of what it means to be a human being.

6 Psychology at war

Even nailed-on warmongers say that all they want is peace. So what is the point of war? I guess it must be good for something because it has been part of human societies since they first appeared. It appears to be an inevitable feature of human societies because whatever time in history you choose to look at, there will be armies marching across some part of the world in an attempt to gain control over another group of people or another territory. It is also fair to say, however, that living peacefully is another inevitable feature of human societies, and we spend much more time at peace than they do at war.

The controversy here is not about the war itself (that is for a different book) but the role of psychology in contributing to and responding to war and its effects. The controversies we will look at in this chapter are

- What can psychology tell us about war? And how does the vision of humanity that psychology presents to us affect the way we respond to war?
- How has psychology been used in warfare?
- What can psychology tell us about the effects of war?
- How has psychology contributed to our understanding of terrorism?

What can psychology tell us about war?

The term war means different things in different contexts. It is worth establishing the view of war that is presented to us in the West before moving on to see how psychology has explained this.

The Western view of war

Most people in the Western world have enjoyed a relatively peaceful existence for the last 50 years or more. We have been able to negotiate serious political difficulties in such a way that large armies have not been mobilised and our countries have not been invaded or attacked. I would argue that this has been achieved by exporting our disputes and conducting them in other parts of the world, but that argument is not really the subject of this text.

DOI: 10.4324/9781003147589-6

The experience of war over the last 50 years has brought us to a point where Western peoples regard war as a specialised activity carried out by expert soldiers with high-tech weapons in a place far away from their own homes. We therefore tend to see war as a dramatic event much like a film, rather than a personal event with real danger for ourselves or our families and property. This is not how warfare was conducted in the past, nor how it is conducted in most parts of the world today. For many people, warfare is a real and ongoing threat to their personal safety.

Over the last 50 years, the Western viewer has been shown images of war that are either amusing (Dad's Army), or heroic (Dunkirk, The Great Escape, Saving Private Ryan). For most people who experience war, however, it is neither amusing nor heroic. It is made up of frightening events, mass death, mass injury, the loss of loved ones and the loss of property and homes. Most recently, it has led to the mass migration of peoples across the world as they struggle to escape from brutal war zones.

The brutality of historical events is illustrated by the Battle of the Somme. On the first of July, 1916, during one day at the Battle of the Somme in the First World War (1914–1918) over 20,000 British troops were slaughtered due to the tactics of their commanders (Taylor, 1963). The troops were required to come out of their trenches carrying heavy equipment and charge towards the enemy trenches where they were cut down by machine gunfire. Not content with this, the tactic was repeated the next day, and for the next four months until the battle was finally brought to end with no obvious strategic advantage but at the cost of 420,000 British casualties. By the end of this war, around one-quarter of all British men of military age had been slaughtered. It is not possible to convey in this text the horror of war and its consequences. We will, however, look at some of the contributions (good and bad) that psychology has made to our understanding of war and the conduct of war.

Is war inevitable?

Are we born to start wars or do we learn to do this? What is it about people that lead us into conflicts that are resolved with mass destruction and mass death? We might start by observing that aggression is an important part of our behaviour and that this attribute has considerable survival value. Aggression, however, is not war. Animals can be aggressive to each other but most of them do not organise into groups to wage an aggressive campaign on another group of the same species. A number of psychologists have looked at the issue of warfare and offered theories about it. In this section, we will briefly look at contributions from William James, William McDougall, Sigmund Freud, John Bowlby and Margaret Mead. The list reads like a Who's Who in the history of psychology, and their contributions give a flavour of the range of ideas that have been put forward to explain this very human activity.

William James and William McDougall were both influential psychologists working in the early years of the 20th century. They had very different political beliefs and these were reflected in their contributions to the topic of war. James was a pacifist and was therefore opposed to all forms of warfare. McDougall, on the other hand, believed in eugenics and so believed that is possible to create genetically superior people through selective breeding (see earlier chapters in this text).

William James

In James' essay 'The Moral Equivalent of War', he set out his analysis of war and how it can be avoided. This essay was written before the First World War (1914–1919) at a time when this conflict was becoming inevitable and when politicians were talking about having a 'war to end all war'. James pointed out how war makes history, and that it is largely described in terms of heroic events even though it is often irrational and far from noble. Early descriptions of warfare, for example, those of the Ancient Greeks, tell of pirate wars of incredible brutality. Groups of men fought for the spoils of another city or island and if they won, they plundered the goods and murdered or enslaved the inhabitants. By the turn of the 20th century, the fight for goods and people was not seen as an adequate justification for war and different arguments were used. One argument that is still used today is that we have to go to war in order to get peace.[1]

   James suggested that wars bring some benefits and he argued that we have to find an equivalent to war that brings about the same benefits. He argued that the military values of strength, bravery, discipline and collective action are the foundation of any successful enduring society. His suggestion of a substitution for war was a mass mobilisation of young men to carry out physical labour and public works for a set number of years. This would encourage all the perceived virtues of military service without war. This view implies that people have certain qualities that have to be addressed through physical action and struggle, and without this struggle, our society will become vulnerable to attack from outside and from within.

The eugenicist

William McDougall's view was not so different in some respects. In his account of 'The Instinct of Pugnacity', he also argued that we are predisposed towards fighting. He argued that it is an important feature in the development of human beings, and he put forward an evolutionary argument that the fittest survive and the weakest are removed. He suggested that this is the main reason that we fight rather than for possessions or for ideals.

   The solution that McDougall proposed was very different to the one suggested by James. McDougall saw warfare as an important aid to the development of a

---

1 Some might argue that fighting for peace is like shagging for virginity, but they would be dangerous radicals.

healthy society. He argued against the liberal idea that an advanced society will find other ways of resolving conflict than through war. He saw the removal of war as a dangerous development that would lead to the degeneration of our society. He therefore argued for natural selection to be re-introduced through another means, that of selective breeding where the fittest and best (presumably including McDougall himself) have more children and the weakest and the worst (fill in the list to your taste) are discouraged from breeding or killed.

The argument for a eugenic solution attracted a lot of support across Europe and the United States during the 1920s and the 1930s. It was taken to its logical and horrific conclusion by the Nazis in Germany during the 1930s until their final defeat in 1945. They dealt with the eugenics issue by murdering people they perceived to be inferior or weak, including the jews, slav and gypsy peoples, homosexuals and the mentally ill. You would think that this horror would close off the eugenic argument but as you have seen elsewhere in this text, it has resurfaced and is unfortunately alive and well.

The psychoanalysts

Freud's thoughts on war are summarised in a letter he wrote to Albert Einstein as part of an academic exchange on the subject (Medoff, 2009). It was written in 1932 when the horror of the killing fields of the First World War was still having an effect on the way people thought and acted. In the letter, he pointed out that aggressive behaviour by one strong individual can only be challenged through collective action. A community can come together and overthrow a tyrant, though it will only avoid a new tyrant if the community stays together and is well organised. These communities can be aggressive towards each other and this is the basis of warfare.

Freud argued that some wars have a positive effect because they establish large empires. In our recorded history these empires have often imposed order within their boundaries and provided a peaceful existence for their citizens. There are, however, a number of unfortunate downsides to large empires, such as the persecution of minorities and the suppression of civil liberties. Freud wondered whether the development of international organisations would allow nations to develop a world order that removed the rationale for warfare. At the time, he was writing the League of Nations (an early version of the United Nations) was attempting, unsuccessfully as it happens, to do just that. Freud suggested that such an organisation needed to have a supreme court and also enough force to enact its judgements. It was on the second point that the League of Nations failed.

John Bowlby put forward another psychoanalytic explanation in a book written with E.F.M. Durbin (Durbin & Bowlby, 1939). They observed that aggression and warfare have been observed in most cultures and at most times of history. They also observed that warfare and aggression form a far smaller proportion of activity than does co-operation. They argue that warfare is just an extension of aggressive behaviours shown by individuals. The primary causes of these behaviours are identical in adults to the causes in children and also animals. The primary causes are to do with

a   Possession: owning property and territory, taking property and territory, and defending it.
b   Frustration: negative feelings when ambitions and desires are blocked.
c   Arrival of strangers: often associated with fear.
d   Attack of a scapegoat: picking on the weak and the outsider.

These four causes are seen as the root of all aggression whether it is between individuals, or groups or even nation-states.

Durbin and Bowlby went on to point out how the defence mechanisms of psychoanalytic theory can be used to explain the features of modern human conflict. For example, fears and hatreds that exist within a group of people can be projected onto a despised group. In this way, the nation-state can show all the aggressive behaviours of an individual.

Although Durbin and Bowlby believed that war is a chronic social disease they did not believe that this disease was incurable. They pointed out that most nations spend far more time in peaceful and cooperative activities than they do at war. The problem then is to strengthen and develop these peaceful impulses and behaviour. It also seems possible that societies can be adjusted so that the people in them do not develop so much aggression.

The anthropologist

Margaret Mead wrote extensively about the customs and behaviour of different peoples around the world. She argued that warfare is not inevitable and not part of our nature, but a human invention (Mead, 1940). She argued that many institutions such as marriage are almost universal amongst peoples but we must have originally lived without marriage and then at some point invented it. She suggested the same is true for warfare and cites evidence from Inuit and Yupik peoples.

In Mead's account, the Inuit are a nomadic people who have no concept of war even though they cannot be described as pacifists. Mead described how fights, theft of wives (!), and murder were a part of their life. What was not part of Inuit life was the organisation of one group of people to maim and kill another group of people. It might be possible to argue that Inuit do not have war because they are nomadic and because they have few possessions. However, to challenge this, Mead presented examples of other nomadic groups with few possessions who have developed all the rituals of warfare.

Mead's account is a little more optimistic than the others in this section because it suggests we are not the victims of our nature. She does, however, point out that once people have invented something they rarely go back and stop using it. The way forward, she suggests is to invent a better way of dealing with conflict than warfare. She observed the development of justice in Western society over the last few hundred years from trial by the ordeal through to trial by jury. People invented new ways of dealing with justice when the old way no longer worked and a better way was available. She suggested the same might be possible for the elimination of warfare.

Summary

The above historical contributions on the nature of human warfare present the view of Western psychology which is largely pessimistic about the future for humanity. The general picture appears to be that war is likely to continue because we have natural tendencies to be aggressive or we have, at least, learnt how effective warfare can be. The theories produce few, if any, testable hypotheses and they focus on whether we are the victims of our biology or whether we are able to shape our own destiny through the development of better ways of living.

These views of war were based on the experience of conflict in the West in the first half of the twentieth century. Since then, the military and economic dominance of the 'Great Powers' means that these conflicts are less likely to occur (let's hope), but armed struggle has taken different forms. This armed struggle that commonly challenges the position of these Big Powers are often characterized as being terrorism. We will come back to this below, but first, we look at the history of psychology in warfare.

How has psychology been used in warfare?

Psychology has been involved in many aspects of warfare for over a hundred years. In this section, I'll try and give you a flavour of that involvement and relate it where possible to psychological concepts and studies from the mainstream of psychology.

Early work in military psychology

Up until the 1960s, military psychology was mainly concerned with the same issues that would concern any major employer of people

- selection of appropriate staff
- matching people (soldiers) to machines
- training (military) specialists
- staff welfare

The selection of the right person for the right job is a concern of any employer, and none more so than the military. In fact, the first mass IQ testing was carried out on the soldiers of the US army during the First World War (1914–1918) and this is described in chapter 5. The testing also marked the start of the extensive military use of psychometric testing for the selection of staff.

On the issue of matching soldiers to machines, it is very important that any machine should be as easy to use as possible and as free from error as possible. For those of you who drive more than one car, you might well have come across a vehicle with the indicator control on the opposite side to your usual vehicle. This means that you keep switching on the window wipers every time you want to turn right. This is not a big problem, but it would be different if pressing the wrong lever didn't turn the wipers on, but instead launched a thermo-nuclear attack on Bournemouth.

An illustration of this problem occurred during the Second World War (1939–1945), and it came about because the military had concentrated on training pilots to fly aircraft rather than designing aircraft that could be flown by pilots. They discovered that even very experienced pilots were prone to make errors with the poorly designed control systems. For example, similar-looking controls operating the landing gear and the steering flaps on some B-25 bombers were placed next to each other. The unfortunate consequence of this was that several B-25s were brought into land without the landing gear in place and so landed on their bellies. The pilots believed that they had activated the landing gear, but in fact they had just steered the plane (Mark, Warm & Huston, 1987). Observations like this led to the development of aircraft controls that more nearly match the capabilities of pilots.

Animals at war

Another area where psychology contributed to military action was in training animals to take part in combat. Most famous amongst these attempts was the work of Skinner (1960) during the Second World War (1939–1945) to train pigeons to navigate missiles to enemy targets. With startling originality, but admirable directness, the programme was called 'Project Pigeon'. This was not the first time, nor the last, that the potential of animals was exploited in warfare. Skinner reported that the British Navy used seagulls to detect submarines in the First World War (1914–1918). The Navy sent its own submarines into the English Channel to release food. This attracted flocks of seagulls who learnt to associate the sight of an underwater vessel with the appearance of food. They would then follow any submarine whether it was British or German. Therefore, a flock of seagulls in the Channel would be the sign of an approaching German submarine. Dogs and dolphins are among the other animals that have been used for military purposes, and the consequences for these animals was often not a good meal, but an early death as the explosives which were attached to them were detonated.

To cut a long, though interesting, story short, Skinner showed that his pigeons could accurately pilot a missile to seek out ships, and could then discriminate between different types of ships so that they could fly past allied ships and dive onto enemy ships. The military got as far as modifying some of their missiles to accommodate the pigeons and their tracking apparatus. However, the pigeons were never brought into active service most likely because the military was uneasy at the thought of heavily armed pigeons flying overhead. Those of you who have ever stood in Trafalgar Square will immediately see the problem.

Military psychology after the 1960s

An article in the American Psychologist by Windle and Vallance (1964) reflected the change that was beginning to take place in military psychology in the

1960s. The article suggested that psychology was turning its attention to para-military issues, for example, studies to investigate the political motivations of guerrilla fighters, the human factors in underground organisations and so on.

It is not possible to give a full account of what is going on in military psychology since, not surprisingly, only a part of it is ever made public. Watson (1980) carried out a thorough review of this work and I recommend his book to you if you are interested to find out more. In his research for the book, he unearthed 7,500 studies around the world sponsored by a range of organisations. He goes on to suggest that many studies do not see the light of day because they are classified as military secrets or have some other restriction put on the information. The following takes a very selective look at some of the issues raised by Watson and others.

The effects of captivity

Watson (1980) describes a study carried out on survivors from Japanese Prisoner of War (POW) camps during the Second World War (1939–1945). The study suggests that the Japanese were unprepared for large numbers of POWs with the result that the guards were allowed to develop their own ways of dealing with the prisoners. The conditions in the camps were crowded and dirty and the food was in short supply. A number of tortures were used in-cluding beatings, standing to attention in the sun for hours, pulling out the hair or fingernails and keeping the POW's eyelids open with sticks and forcing them to look at the sun for hours.

The prisoners avoided talk and thought of home because this was too painful. Instead, they talked about the work they had to do and the food they might eat. Internal discipline declined and food was often stolen. Depression and anxiety were common initial responses though they were often replaced by a lack of emotional responses to the point where the prisoners were unable to laugh or cry. Another common effect of captivity and hunger was a range of cognitive deficits including difficulty in concentration and loss of memory. Many soldiers remained in the camps for years until the end of the war, and many others did not survive the experience.

The general conclusions of this and many other studies are that the reactions to captivity are affected by two main factors; the physical hardships of the confinement and the unpredictable and cruel behaviour of the guards.

The Stanford prison experiment

This brings us to a famous study in social psychology by Zimbardo (see Haney, Banks & Zimbardo, 1973) on the psychological effects of captivity. This work is has created a lot of interest over the years and has been reviewed and debated extensively (Zimbardo, 2007; Banyard 2007, Reicher & Haslam, 2006). In this study, a number of young, healthy males were kept in a mock prison in the basement of the Stanford University Psychology Department. The captivity produced such dramatic effects that the study had the be stopped after only 6 days to prevent further psychological harm to the participants. This study is often described in the context of civilian prisons but it is possible to see it in a very different light. The study was funded by the US Navy and many of the features of the experiment did not correspond to the experience of people taken to prison after breaking the law.

The differences from the civilian prison experience included

- The surprise arrest of the participants and their immediate imprisonment. This is more like the experience of a hostage or a POW rather than a criminal.
- The depersonalisation of the prisoners through clothing and changes in their appearance. Prisoners in Western jails are commonly not depersonalised in this way.
- The freedom of the guards to develop their own procedures and to apply their own rules as they liked. Again this is more the experience of the hostage or POW than the criminal.
- The prisoners were referred to by their number only, whereas in Western jails they are referred to by name as well as number. POWs on the other hand are often referred to by number alone.

You might think that it is unlikely that the US Navy had any interest in the running of civilian prisons but it did have an interest in preparing its personnel to deal with captivity and cope with the inevitable stress of such an experience. More recently, however, the US military did in fact take over the running of prisons during its occupation of Iraq with disastrous results (see below).

Interrogation techniques

Prisoners are interrogated mainly when someone believes that they have information of value to the captors. The prisoners might well be under instruction to disclose nothing, and therefore the captor might employ a range of techniques to encourage disclosure. In many armies, it is a military offence to collaborate with the enemy, and soldiers who talk too readily are prosecuted when they return home. Many of the interrogation techniques involve pain or discomfort, though they have only a limited effect. A lot of interest has centred on ways of making people more talkative using psychological techniques.

One of the most prominent of these techniques is sensory deprivation. This involves reducing the amount of perceptual stimulation that a person has to a minimum. This might involve solitary confinement in a warm room with low or no light and little or no sound. Some people find this very stressful, and most people find that it creates some sensory distortions. Watson (1980) refers to the extensive work carried out in this field for the American and Canadian military starting with the studies of Donald Hebb. He reports how, under sensory deprivation conditions, people often experienced hallucinations, an inability to distinguish between sleep and wakefulness and a distortion in their sense of time. Moreover, when they were released from the sensory deprivation they often felt overwhelmed by the colours and noises of everyday life, felt light-headed and were rather talkative (key point this). The sensory deprivation studies included investigations on the effects of the experience on conformity to group pressure and response to propaganda.

A variation on the sensory deprivation technique was used by the British Army in Northern Ireland in the early days of The Troubles. Shallice (1973) reported on 12 internees who were subjected to a horrifying interrogation technique. In the gaps between direct interrogation, the men were hooded in a black woven bag, subjected to very loud white noise and forced to stand against a wall with their hands above their heads. They were required to stand there for up to 16 hours and if they moved they were beaten. The internees were required to wear loose boiler suits, was sleep deprived and put on a restricted diet. This treatment had a devastating effect on the men who had major physical, cognitive, and emotional responses.

Overall, it would appear from the range of studies carried out that disorientation of prisoners is effective in increasing their willingness to talk. This disorientation can be achieved through, among other means, unpredictable torture, sleep deprivation, drugs, hunger and sensory deprivation. These techniques are now known to have long-term consequences for the mental health of the people subjected to them.

The involvement of psychology with techniques that many would think constitute torture clearly cuts across the ethical standards of the profession. The argument for the participation in torture by psychologists is that it supports their country and its presumed moral purpose to fight for peace, fight against terror (pick your own justification). There are also, of course, many arguments against the involvement of psychologists in combat activities. We go on to discuss this further later in the chapter but not before we have looked at some of the human consequences of war.

On killing

You'd think that battlefields are murderous places but the history of warfare shows that in many battles far fewer deaths occur than you'd expect given the number of people there and the firepower available. Studies from the Second World War (1936–1945) provided an explanation for this. Marshall (1974) found that fewer than 20% of US riflemen would fire at an enemy. The soldiers who didn't fire did not run and hide and were willing to risk death and injury to support colleagues or to get ammunition. They just would not fire at another human being. This observation was corroborated by the US Airforce who concluded that most of its fighter pilots would not fire at an enemy plane.

Looking back to an earlier conflict, the Battle of Gettysburg of 1863 is often described as the turning point in the American Civil War and produced the greatest number of casualties of any battle in this conflict. After the battle, over

25,000 muskets were recovered from the battlefield. Of these, around 90% were loaded which is quite surprising. Much more surprising, however, was the observation that 12,000 of the muskets were found to be loaded more than once and 6,000 had three or more shots in them, and one musket had been loaded 23 times without firing. It took ages to load a musket and no time at all to fire it. You'd expect most of the muskets to be unloaded. The obvious conclusion is that man soldiers were not firing at the enemy. They wanted to look as if they were firing so maybe they held the musket to their shoulder, pretended to fire and then filled it up again. These soldiers would go against all their training and not fire at the enemy. They did not want to kill another human being (Grossman, 1995).

The realization that the majority of their soldiers did not fire at an enemy and apparently allow their humanity to trump their training was a problem for military commanders who want their soldiers to be efficient killing machines. Unwitting help was at hand, however, from psychology. The famous studies of Stanley Milgram (1974) showed that he could create a situation where the majority of people would follow simple orders and kill another human being (in case you don't know the studies, they didn't really kill them). The Western military was all over these studies and changed their training to introduce various psychology techniques. By the time, the United States was fighting in Vietnam, their fire rate had increased to 90% (Grossman, 1995) and the US army now had its efficient killing machine. They still lost that war, however.

Summary

The above gives a flavour of some of the issues in the application of psychology to warfare. There are numerous other issues that have been investigated including, how soldiers behave in groups, what makes a good military leader, what are the effects of being under fire, and why do some soldiers commit atrocities. All of these issues and many more have attracted a lot of interest from various military organisations, and as long as wars continue in different parts of the world they will have loads of material for their research and many applications for the findings of that research.

What can psychology tell us about the effects of war?

One of the clearest summaries of the effects of war is contained in the report on nuclear war written by the British Psychological Society (Thompson, 1985). The report was written to review the best psychological evidence available on all aspects of nuclear war. It appears a little dated now because there no longer seems to be a threat of full-scale nuclear war between two large and heavily armed countries, but it does still have much to say about the consequences of war. It considered responses to previous wars and natural disasters so as to build up a picture of how people would deal with large scale destruction and mass civilian casualties. The report can be used in the planning of civil defence so that we can be better prepared to deal with disastrous events.

Post-traumatic stress disorder

One of the effects of war that has been extensively studied by psychologists is the condition known as post-traumatic stress disorder (PTSD). The concept of this condition grew out of work in many different fields of traumatic stress, for example, the condition referred to as 'shell shock' during the First World War. It took a long time, however, for the condition to be actually recognised as a syndrome in its own right, and for the military, as well as others, to realise that it was actually a debilitating condition resulting from traumatic experiences, and not just cowardliness or an over-vivid imagination.

The experience of post-traumatic stress is not confined to combatants. Waugh (1997) looked at the impact of the Second World War (1939–1945) on women civilians. Many of these experienced war at first hand, especially if they lived in the major cities that experienced heavy bombing. Some of these women showed the same type of intrusive thoughts and avoidance found in combatants with PTSD. The diagnosis of PTSD is discussed in more detail in Chapter 4.

The Minnesota starvation studies

One of the effects of war and sometimes the experience of captivity is starvation. In one of the most remarkable studies in psychology, Ancel Keys and his colleagues at the University of Minnesota (Keys et al., 1950) studied this process by recruiting healthy volunteers to experience starvation. The experiment involved restricting the food intake of 36 young, healthy, psychologically stable men who had volunteered for the study as an alternative to military service. The study took place during the Second World War and many of the volunteers were conscientious objectors. For the first three months, they ate normally while their behaviour, personality, and eating patterns were studied in detail. For the next six months, they were restricted to about half of their regular food intake and so dropped in weight, on average, by around 25%. The final three months of the study was a rehabilitation phase during which the men gradually returned to their normal diet.

The individual responses of the men were very varied but the overall pattern is one of the substantial changes in their physical, psychological, emotional and social responses. And some of these changes continued through the rehabilitation phase and beyond.

The changes included a preoccupation with food and the development of complex rituals for consuming food. Conversation became very focused on food and mealtimes became extended as the food was consumed slower and slower. Several of the men reported episodes where they broke their diet and binged which was followed by sickness (sometimes self-generated) and then self-reproach. During the rehabilitation phase, many of the volunteers ate massive meals and, on average, not only achieved their original body weight but increased it by a further 10%.

The physical changes were striking and the men came to resemble the skeletal pictures we have seen of prisoners and victims of war. Their metabolism slowed, their blood volume dropped and their hearts shrank. In all the volunteers, their eyeballs became unnaturally white. Despite all these changes, the men did not see themselves as being excessively skinny. In fact, they began to think that everyone else looked too fat, rather than they themselves being too thin.

The emotional changes were equally dramatic with many becoming irritable and prone to angry outbursts. Apathy was commonly observed, and some men who had been well presented neglected various aspects of personal hygiene. Most of the participants experienced periods during which their emotional distress was quite severe, with at least one volunteer being admitted to a psychiatric facility. Their social behaviour was also dramatically changed. If you are interested to read more, then check out the original study or search for the Minnesota Starvation Studies.

These studies give us clear evidence of the dramatic effects on human beings of having a restricted diet. You might have some concerns about the ethics of the study and to be fair you would be right. What we can take from this is that the many people we see displaced by war and famine around the world are dealing with these physical, emotional and psychological effects of reduced diets.

Summary

We are becoming increasingly aware of how war can have damaging psychological effects on civilians as well as the combatants. One of the controversies that this work provokes is whether we should try and help people with stress reactions so that they can deal more effectively with war (and therefore maybe prolong it), or whether psychology should encourage people to deal with the stress by opposing war and so reducing the opportunities for the stress occurring in future generations.

Psychology and the war on terror

One person's terrorist is another person's freedom fighter. It's all a matter of context. And what do you call it when a fighter plane is used to fire missiles at civilians on their way home from prayers, killing a religious leader in his wheelchair along with seven others (The Guardian, 2004)? I'd call that state terrorism but that is commonly not how such news is presented to us. Many Western governments use extreme and deadly force to maintain their influence and control over various parts of the world. However, as commonly presented to the public in the West, terror is what THEY do to us, not what WE do to them.

Terrorism is defined in the United States by the Department of Homeland Security as 'the unlawful use of force and violence against persons or property to intimidate or coerce a government, the civilian population, or any segment thereof, in furtherance of political or social objectives' (FBI). This department was set up after the attack on the World Trade Centre in New York on 11th September 2001. Those with longer memories might apply this definition to the other September 11 attacks in 1973, when a US—backed military coup overthrew the elected government of Chile in a revolution that claimed over 3000 lives and installed a regime of terror for the next two decades.

It is very difficult to provide an academic or indeed a coherent political definition of terrorism (Blackbourne, 2011; Bryan et al., 2011). What is undeniable though is that around the world military groups, state-sponsored and otherwise, use techniques to create terror in pursuit of their military and material goals. Most remarkably, and without irony, President George W Bush launched a War on Terror which has itself brought unimaginable terror to the peoples of Afghanistan and the Middle East. Untold numbers of people have died in this war and millions have been displaced. The issue for this book is to consider some of psychology's contribution to these actions.

Psychologists at Guantanamo Bay

In 2002, the United States set up a prison camp outside of its home territory, and therefore outside US law, to house the people it was capturing (kidnapping?) around the world who they believed were terrorists. President Bush said these people were not soldiers and hence not subject to the protection offered by the Geneva Convention. In some cases, the people were taken from conflict zones in Afghanistan and Pakistan and in some cases they were snatched from countries where there was no conflict. Some were taken through UK facilities on their way to Guantanamo.

To describe the full horror of Guantanamo would take a book in itself and if you want to know more about it then just search the internet. The issue we want to look at in this book is the role of psychologists at Guantanamo and also at other modern military prisons. The role of Guantanamo was not just to contain these people but to get information from them about possible attacks on Western countries and so interrogation techniques were very important. This is where psychologists come in and one of the many techniques that were able to bring along was sensory deprivation (see above). If you look at the image in Figure 6.1 you will see prisoners at Guantanamo in orange jumpsuits. If you look closer you will see that they have earmuffs (so they can't hear anything), opaque glasses (so they can see anything) and thick gloves (so they can't feel anything). This is sensory deprivation. And they have shackles on their ankles and wrists, that's why they appear to be praying.

The involvement of psychologists in military interrogation created a storm through the profession. In most people's eyes, the interrogation of people who

Figure 6.1 Sensory deprivation at Guantanamo Bay.

are being held outside international law (in other words illegally) is unethical in itself, but to then subject them to inhuman treatment can be classed as torture and to continue with this over a period of years is beyond description. There does not appear to be an ethical dilemma here because it is clearly wrong, or is it?

The use of health professionals including psychologists in abusive interrogation techniques is now well documented (e.g., Soldz, 2007). The interrogations at Guantanamo were overseen by a Behavioural Science Consultation Team (BSCT) which included psychologists (Lifton, 2004) and the team prepared psychological profiles for the interrogators to use. It is also clear that '*since late 2002 ... psychologists have been part of a strategy that employs extreme stress, combined with behaviour shaping rewards, to extract actionable intelligence from resistant captives*' (Bloche & Marks, 2005, p. 6).

PsyOps

At the same time as Guantanamo was operating, the United States was taking charge of a military prison in Baghdad during the invasion of Iraq. The military brought to the Abu Ghraib prison the techniques they had developed at Guantanamo (Soldz, 2007) and psychologists were at the forefront of this operation. This prison hit the news when pictures of the degrading treatment being inflicted on the inmates were sent to a newspaper. Some junior soldiers were tried and imprisoned for this but their commanders were not. In interviews, the guards described how they were responding to what they perceived to be the requests of PsyOps units (Psychological Operations). One of those charged, Private Lynndie England, who featured prominently in the first batch of photographs and was subsequently jailed, insisted she was acting on orders from *'persons in my chain of command'; 'I was instructed by persons in higher rank to "stand there, hold this leash, look at the camera', and they took pictures for PsyOps'* (see, for example, Ronson, 2005).

The ethics of interrogation

In 2002, just as Guantanamo was coming on line, the American Psychological Association (APA) made a change in its ethical code. This change concerned situations where a psychologist comes into conflict between the orders they are being given and their ethical code. So for example, if they were a member of the military and were asked to carry out an inhumane interrogation which is against the ethical code of psychologists, what should they do? Should they go with their ethical code or should they follow their orders? This is an easy decision when sitting in a comfy chair reading a book and much harder one in a real-life situation.

The response of the APA could have been to put pressure on the military and the US Government not to carry out torture and not to require psychologists to be part of it. What they did, however, was to change their ethical code to give psychologists a get-out clause and take part in the torture. The new code said,

> If the conflict is unresolvable [between orders and ethics] psychologists may adhere to the requirements of the law, regulations, or other governing legal authority.
>
> (APA 2002)

This addition to the APA ethics code hit a nerve in the United States and the United Kingdom because it is an echo of the Nuremberg Defence. This is the moral defence for war crimes that says *'it wasn't my fault, I was obeying orders'*. It is called the Nuremberg Defence because it was used by the people who were put on trial for war crimes after the Second World War (1939–1945). The defence was rejected at those trials so it made it all the more controversial to add this defence to the APA ethical code.

The APA was put under intense pressure over its stance and eventually sent a delegation to look at the Guantanamo facility led by the then-president Ronald Levant who wrote,

> I accepted this invitation to visit Guantanamo because I saw it as an important opportunity for the Association to provide input on the question of how psychologists can play an appropriate and ethical role in national security investigations.
>
> (Levant, 2007, p. 2)

He was accompanied on the trip by Steven Sharfstein, President of the American Psychiatric Association, who was so alarmed by what he en-countered that he called for all psychiatrists to have nothing more to do with military interrogations. No such clear statement came from the APA and the involvement of psychologists continued at military interrogation facilities.

Most revealing in Levant's description of what he encountered at Guantanamo is the following,

> We next visited the brand new psychiatric wing, which has both inpatient and outpatient services. I had a very unusual experience as we were standing at the nursing station, receiving a briefing from the psychiatrist. Behind me a voice asked "Dean Levant? Is that you?" That was the last thing I expected to hear at GTMO! I turned to see a former doctoral student in clinical psychology from Nova Southeastern University (NSU), who is now a military psychologist. I thought to myself, "NSU's graduates sure have done a good job of getting out into the world!"
>
> (Levant, 2007, p. 5)

Study psychology, see the world and use sensory deprivation techniques on kidnap victims. It's a catchy slogan, but it might not attract the business that psychology wants.

Finally, in 2009 there was a change of government in the United States and President Obama brought in a new attitude to Guantanamo and clearly stated that he did not want Americans involved in torture. The APA also changed its line and amended its ethical code as follows;

> The APA Ethics Committee will not accept any defense to torture in its adjudication of ethics complaints. Torture in any form, at any time, in any place, and for any reason, is unethical for psychologists and wholly inconsistent with membership in the American Psychological Association.
>
> (APA, 2009)

This all sounds like a very negative story about psychology and psychologists and it is obviously not the profession's finest hour. However, during the time that Guantanamo was operational many psychologists kept up a barrage of articles that challenged the APA's position and some decided to leave the APA (e.g., Pope and Gutheil, 2009). The debate about ethics was kept going throughout this time and eventually the APA arrived at a result that was in agreement with other similar professions such as doctors and psychiatrists.

Summary

Psychology has been used as a weapon of war across the world. The examples we have looked at mainly concern the actions of the US military. This is not because the Americans are the only people to use these tactics, nor are they by any stretch of the imagination the worst, but they are the most reported and recorded army anywhere and so the information is readily available.

There are two big moral questions here. First, is it ever appropriate for psychologists to support military action? We might argue that the use of psychology can reduce injury or the loss of life. Anything that speeds up a conflict will bring nearer the time of peace. We might also argue that some conflicts are morally justified and therefore it is appropriate to use psychology to advance the cause. It is also worth pointing that much of the work of military psychologists are in the management of service personnel and their care and protection. Psychology has a lot to say about the response of combatants and civilians to warfare and can make some valuable contributions (Summerfield, 2000).

The second question that arises if you answer yes to the first one is, what are the limits of that action? This is the more taxing challenge because psychologists who decide to take part in military activity still have to draw lines that set limits on their engagement. It is also fair to say that those of us who decide not to take part, still enjoy the benefits of living in a successful and militarily powerful society, so we can't just wash our hands of it and protest our innocence. We are complicit in these actions.

7   Psychology and persuasion

Politicians, advertisers, religious leaders and even your mum try to influence what you think and what you do through persuasive messaging. The controversy arises around the nature of these messages and the role of psychologists in designing and delivering messages that are deceptive and coercive. In this chapter, we start by looking at the history of propaganda before moving on to look at the use of big data to nudge us into behavioural change.

Propaganda and persuasive messages

What is propaganda?

There is no simple definition of propaganda because your judgement of a message depends on what attitudes you hold to start with. If you agree with a political message you might view it as a statement of fact, but if you do not agree with it you might see it as manipulative propaganda. The following sections explore some of the key features of persuasive messages and propaganda using examples from two military conflicts of the 20th century. We will then go on to look at some of the techniques used by politicians in their attempt to get us to agree with them. First, we will start by looking at what we mean by propaganda and persuasive messages.

Propaganda and education

The word propaganda is derived from the Latin word propagare which refers to a gardener's practice of pinning fresh shoots of a plant into the earth so that they grow and become separate plants. So, if we take it literally, propaganda means 'that which is to be spread'. The term was first used in its modern sense by the Catholic church during the 17th century to describe the spread of Christianity. This was thought to be a good thing if you were a Catholic (but a bad thing if you were not a Catholic), and the people conducting the propaganda did not see their work as devious or underhand. Today, though, the term has some very sinister connotations.

There is an overlap between propaganda and education. Both activities try to inform people and change people, but one we see as a generally good thing,

DOI: 10.4324/9781003147589-7

Table 7.1 Distinctions between propaganda and education

	Education	Propaganda
Aims		
1	Change attitudes	Change feelings
2	Change factual and verifiable beliefs	Change beliefs about matters of taste or unverifiable issues
Motives		
3	The source of the message is disinterested and does not stand to gain from the acceptance of the message	The source is prejudiced and stands to profit from the success of his communication
4	The source does not intend to deceive	The source intends to deceive
Content		
5	Correct information and rational argument	Incorrect or selective information and emotional argument
Effect		
6	Impact comes about through the receiver's attention and comprehension	Impact is determined by the receiver yielding
7	Retention	Action

and the other we deny having anything to do with. McGuire (1973) makes a number of distinctions between education and propaganda (see Table 7.1), though it is fair to say that many messages fall between the two sets of criteria.

When we think of propaganda one of the first images that comes to mind is that of posters designed to help 'the war effort', or in other words to encourage people to accept the war that is taking place, accept the sacrifices they are making and to work harder. An example from Second World War (1939–1945) is shown in Figure 7.1. One of the common themes of British propaganda at this time were atrocity stories about the behaviour of the enemy. The aim of these images was to encourage people to continue the fight by suggesting (a) we must not let these bad people win, and (b) we are the good guys and we are fighting for a good cause (it is a just war). Rumours circulated about the Germans, for example, that they boiled the corpses of enemy soldiers to make soap. Some of the atrocity stories had a small amount of truth, though others were entirely made up (Pratkanis & Aronson, 1992). This process of demonising the enemy, however, that is defined by a government, is still alive and well though usually conducted with a bit more subtlety.

Propaganda was a major concern of social scientists during the 1960s and 1970s. Propaganda was seen as being carried out by THEM – the bad guys (who were usually the communist countries of China and the Soviet Union and their allies) and education was conducted by US the good guys (Europe and the United States and their allies). It was believed that propaganda could have a dramatic effect on people and encourage them to believe in extreme political philosophies and carry out morally indefensible behaviour. The most

Figure 7.1 Example of an 'atrocity story' propaganda message.

powerful means of propaganda was thought to be delivered through large rallies, stirring speeches, controlled television messages and a structured curriculum in schools. It is no longer appropriate to think about propaganda in this way for two reasons, first there is little evidence that it ever had much effect (McGuire, 1985), and second, we receive information in different ways today, particularly through television, radio and social media which are very difficult for any government to control. The current fear is about the radicalisation of young people and we will come back to that below.

Persuasive messages

As we have already seen, it is difficult to consistently distinguish between propaganda and education, and this is one of the reasons that social psychology tends to consider this within the wider issue of persuasive messages. Many of the activities that used to be called propaganda are now called 'news management'. The change of the term is a piece of propaganda in itself. By using a neutral term such as 'news management' rather than the slightly sinister term 'propaganda' the activity takes on a different light to the point where politicians, business people, university Vice Chancellors and the military might boast about their news management successes. News management is a more subtle process than propaganda but the two share a lot of features in common and we can put them both under the heading of persuasive messages. We now move on to look at some of the psychological research that provides a framework for considering persuasive messages.

The Yale research on persuasive communication

The early work on persuasive messages was carried out by Carl Hovland (1953) and his associates at Yale University. Hovland took the approach of learning theory and believed that a message will change a person's attitude or behaviour if the person believes they will obtain some reinforcement from the change. That reinforcement could, for example, be the approval of important people or it could be financial.

The Yale group identified some key stages in this process of change:

1   Exposure: The target of the message must see or hear it for the message to have any influence. Although this sounds incredibly obvious, it is difficult to ensure that target groups actually receive messages.
2   Attention: Once they are exposed to the message, the target must pay attention to it, and with many political messages this is difficult because as soon as the words 'This is a party political broadcast on behalf of .....' the channel has already been changed.
3   Comprehension: The target does not need to understand everything that is said in the message but they must understand the conclusion if it is going to influence them.
4   Acceptance: Once they've understood the message, they have to accept it if change is to take place.
5   Retention: The target does not need to remember the message but they do need to hang on to the new attitude.
6   Change in behaviour: The new attitude has to be one that guides behaviour if the desired result of behavioural change is to be achieved.

Research on the Yale approach

A lot of research was carried out on the effect of messages on attitudes and behaviour though it is beyond the scope of this text to review it in full. Two examples of the work will give a flavour of it, first the sleeper effect and second the selective attention we apply to political messages.

The sleeper effect was first described by Hovland et al. (1949) who noticed that the source of the message had a big effect on how it was received. If the source of the message was respected, then the message had a much greater initial impact that if the source was not respected. For example, a message from a respected politician will have a bigger effect than a message from a drunk man in a public bar. This effect diminished over time, however, and the effect of the respected source declined while the effect of the unrespected source increased. It appeared that people remembered the message and forgot the source. So, if you sleep on it, the message will have a different effect on you, and the influence of the source will diminish. Subsequent research challenged this finding and it appears that the sleeper effect only occurs under certain conditions. Pratkanis et al. (1988) found that the sleeper effect will occur if (a) the message is more memorable than the source, and (b) the message would have been persuasive in the first place if it were not for the unrespected source.

On the issue of attention to messages, it is now an established finding that we tune in to messages we want to hear and messages that we agree with, and tune out of messages we disagree with. As early as 1960 during the first televised Presidential Debates in the US elections, it was observed that viewers would pay attention when their preferred candidate was speaking (either Kennedy or Nixon) but would look away or do something else when the other candidate was speaking (Sigel, 1964). The Yale research produced many findings that are used today by, for example, politicians, advertisers and health educators.

Radicalisation

A recent concern has been the recruitment of (mainly) young people into organisations with views that oppose mainstream Western societies and engage in military activities that are characterised as being terrorist. In this case, the persuasive messages are seen to be targeted at individuals rather than broadcast to the population. Written before the 9/11 attack in New York, and re-markably prophetic of that action, is a report written for the US government of the psychology and sociology of terrorism (Hudson, 1999). This is available on the internet if you are interested in how Western governments frame these views and actions.

An issue for us to confront is why some people will decide to take their own lives, along with random members of the public, in the name of a cause they believe to be just. And what was the process that encouraged them to join radical groups. Mohammad Sidique Khan (see Figure 7.2) was a 30-year-old British-born man from Dewsbury in West Yorkshire. He is believed to have been the leader of the London Bombs attack of 2005 in which 52 people died and 700 were injured as a result of four coordinated explosions. His part in this was to detonate a suicide vest while travelling on the Circle Line near Edgeware Road killing six people and injuring 120. Khan was a family man who was part of his community and worked as a teaching assistant in a local

Figure 7.2 Mohammad Sidique Khan pictured just before the attack on London.

primary school. From initially being quite westernised, he became interested in the Islamic faith before becoming involved in groups and training programmes with people committed to an armed struggle. After his death, among the items left behind by Khan was a handwritten note, with no date, for his wife and daughter. It read: 'Sorry I can't be there, hope you understand. I love you all and inshallah [God willing] will meet you the best of places Jannah [heaven]' (BBC, 2011).

The journey that these young people go along is not clear, and so Western security services are scrambling to work out the motivation for these journeys and to find ways to stop them. The controversy for psychology is where to position itself in this activity. If it frames the question in terms of how much psychologists know about terrorism (e.g., Silke, 2004) then it is already standing with the security services and framing the debate inside the Western tent. From a different viewpoint, these actions are heroic and justifiable. In my opinion, it is that viewpoint that needs exploring before we can hope to understand and prevent these actions.

Psychology can contribute to our understanding of why people decide, like Siddique Khan to become a suicide bomber (e.g., Marsden & Attia, 2005), and also the response of the population to events like this (e.g., Rubin et al., 2005). In the context of this chapter, though, the question is about messaging and how the techniques of using persuasive messages to a whole population have been refined and targeted.

There are numerous sites on the internet that give advice on how to spot grooming and radicalisation (e.g., British Council), and some institutions in the United Kingdom such as universities are required to police and support the Prevent Agenda (see gov.uk, 2021). If psychologists and universities position themselves as agents of the state and the status quo, then the decisions are easy and they can follow the guidance given by the government. But a different position sees that there are a lot of reasons why people might want to follow radical ideas and radical solutions. The planet is being burnt to a cinder in front of our eyes, institutional racism is endemic in the United Kingdom and people from historically marginalised groups are being systematically discriminated against. I could go on, but you see why psychologists have a decision to make about how they frame their questions and conduct their research.

Summary

Psychology has a long history of involvement in designing, delivering and analysing persuasive messages. In some circumstances, it is possible to see the benefits to society from these messages (e.g., health programmes), but there are also clear examples of how messages can be used to further the interests of powerful elites at the expense of the general population (yes, you Mark Zuckerberg). We go on now to look at two examples of wartime campaigns.

Examples of propaganda campaigns

1 American propaganda campaigns in South-East Asia

It is hard to say when the war in Vietnam started. In 1945, Ho Chi Minh proclaimed the Democratic Republic of Vietnam and initiated the final struggle to get rid of the French colonial rulers from his country. Interestingly, he looked to the United States as a friend of this new republic and used the words of the Declaration of Independence of the United States of America in his speech. The French were finally driven out 10 years later but not before the United States had started to become involved against the democratic as- pirations of the Vietnamese people. This involvement was gradually increased and a military government that was favourable to the United States was es- tablished in the South of the country.

For a ten-year period in the mid-1960s and 1970s, the United States waged full-scale war against the Vietnamese people. To this day, it is not clear why they did it. The war ended in 1975 when the Americans were finally driven out of the country by the peasant army of the Vietnamese. At least 1,300,000 people were killed in the conflict and many thousands more were maimed. Of the dead, 58,022 were Americans (less than 5%), the rest were Vietnamese (Pilger, 1989). It is one of the triumphs of Western propaganda that this war is seen today as America's tragedy. Our view of this conflict is seen through the eyes of the Americans and we rarely hear the voice of the Vietnamese people telling us how a poorly armed, rural people managed to endure mass destruction, saturation bombing, extensive use of chemical weapons and mass murder, and go on to defeat the greatest fighting force on the planet.

The Americans had a different propaganda problem in Vietnam to the ones they had encountered before. They could not target their efforts at the Vietnamese fighters since they could never find them, so leaflet drops were carried out on a grand scale. They also directed their attention onto the civilian population so that they would stop supporting the Vietnamese fighters. The Vietnamese fighters also used propaganda techniques though they did not have the same level of resources at their disposal.

A review of the propaganda campaigns of the United States during Vietnam by Watson (1980) suggests that great efforts were made to encourage defection by the Vietnamese fighters. He quotes from military papers which estimate that during the month of March in 1969 the Americans dropped 713 million leaflets, and distributed a further three million by hand all trying to encourage defection. During the same month, 156,000 posters were distributed and 2,000 hours of broadcasting were used for the same purpose. The military report does not estimate the effectiveness of this campaign but does note that the best way to encourage defection was through the stories of fighters who had already defected. These campaigns were planned and organised by psychological operations units (Psy-Ops).

Psy-Ops

A first-hand account of psychological warfare activities during this period was given by the journalist John Pilger who made several trips to Vietnam. The following is one of his diary entries.

> Over Fire Base "Snuffy", Tay Ninh province, South Vietnam, August 30, 1970. "You could say the helicopter has been our salvation in this war," says Captain Frank Littlewood, from Cleveland Ohio. "why, you could say that without the helicopter we wouldn't be doing so damm well in this war!" Captain Littlewood is a Psy-Ops officer of the U.S. First Air Cavalry Division whose colours include the crossed swords of Colonel Custer's Seventh Cavalry. Psy-Ops means Psychological Warfare.

> "What we're doing today," shouts Captain Littlewood over the noise of the rotors, "is psyching out the enemy. We're going to play a tape we call Wandering Soul. Now you've got to understand the Vietnamese way of life to realise the power behind Wandering Soul. You see, the Vietnamese people worship their ancestors and they take a lot of notice of the spirits and stuff like that. Well, what we're going to do is fly low over the jungle and broadcast the voices of ancestors – you know, ghosts – which we've

simulated in our studios. Got it? These ghosts – these ancestors, I mean – are going to tell the Vietcong to stop messing with people's rights to live freely, or they're going to disown them."

Our helicopter drops to a few hundred feet above the trees. Captain Littlewood throws a switch and a reverberating voice emits from two loudspeakers. While the voice reverberates and occasionally hoots, a sergeant hurls out handfuls of leaflets which also offer ancestral threats. Captain Littlewood himself hurls out one unopened box of leaflets. "Maybe," he says, "I'll hit one of them on the head and we won't have to worry about changing his mind."

(Pilger, 1975, pp. 70–71)

Pilger also describes a number of other missions by Psy-Ops forces including one to encourage villagers to support the Americans by giving them tooth-brushes and a chemical toilet. The aim of these missions was to win the hearts and minds of the civilian population, though it has to be said that at the start of these missions the village would be surrounded by heavily armed troops and then fortified with barbed wire. This probably acted as an encouragement for the Vietnamese people to brush their teeth vigorously.

Cultural profiling

Watson (1980) suggests that the above programmes were typical of Psy-Op propaganda tactics that tried to use the cultural beliefs and practices of their enemy to demoralize them. He quotes military documents that show a social profile drawn up on a range of countries. These profiles included such information as,

- prestigious people,
- common gifts used by people to get to know each other,
- waste and disposal patterns,
- attitudes to leaders,
- the opinions of these leaders.

They also collected information on social and religious customs including such items as what smells each culture found most offensive. The propaganda tactic was then to target particular attitudes, particular prominent people and particular customs and beliefs. One example of this approach was the wandering soul's campaign witnessed by Pilger (see above), another one concerned the grieving practices of the Vietnamese. It was the Vietnamese custom to remember deaths after 49 days and after 100 days as well as on anniversaries. Leaflets were dropped by the Americans on these dates after big battles in areas where people would have been likely to have lost relatives. The aim was to increase the misery of those days and further undermine the morale of the Vietnamese.

The above two examples are among the more understandable of the propaganda campaigns. There were others that were less easy to comprehend. For
example, during the Korean war, the Americans collected information on
graffiti in North Korean toilets. The study found very little political graffiti but
it did find occasions where the toilet paper was a newspaper with a picture of
the Korean Leader (Kim Il-Sung). The use of his picture in this way was
strictly forbidden. It was decided to encourage this use by preparing toilet
paper with the picture of Kim Il-Sung on the sheets to encourage .... I'm not
sure what.

2 The Gulf War of 1991

The Gulf War was a very different conflict from the example above. In the
summer of 1990, Iraq invaded and annexed its neighbouring country of
Kuwait. Under the political umbrella of the United Nations, a large armed
forced led by the United States massed in Saudi Arabia and finally in 1991
attacked the Iraqi forces and forced them out of Kuwait. News management,
in this case, was used specifically to keep the civilian populations of the at-
tacking countries happy and in general agreement with the attack.

One of the themes of the comments made by British and American politicians was to associate Saddam Hussain (the leader of Iraq) with Adolf Hitler.
One of the effects of associating two problems together is that it draws you to
look for similar solutions to the problem. The general wisdom about the war
with Germany and Hitler was that the Allies initially made the initial mistake
of appeasing the German dictator when they should have opposed him. The
lesson from history, therefore, is to oppose the dictators and not to appease
them. Laboratory studies by Gilovich (1981) showed that when people were
asked to make hypothetical decisions about a political crisis, one of the key
variables that affected their decision was whether the information they were
given made references to Nazi Germany or if it made references to the
Vietnam conflict. The simple lesson that is often drawn from the Vietnam war
is that America (or any other major power) should not get involved in a
foreign conflict that it has little primary interest in. The people who were
given material with links to Nazi Germany were more likely to favour military
action than the people who were given material with links to the
Vietnam war.

One of the ways to encourage the British and American public to accept
military action against Iraq was to associate the conflict with Second World
War rather than Vietnam. The strategy appeared to work in the first instance,
but it created problems for the Allies at the end of the conflict. The military
campaign ended without taking over the whole of Iraq and without removing
Saddam Hussain from power. It is not possible to imagine the end of the
Second World War without the removal of Adolf Hitler and the Nazi government from power. The analogy broke down for the Gulf War as it became
clear that the Allies did not see Saddam Hussain as Adolf Hitler. Pratkanis and

Aronson (1992) suggested that this realisation marked the start of the decline in popularity of the American President, George Bush (the first).

This focus on the Hitler narrative is still around in the 21st century. We have a constant barrage of news stories that commemorate some activity or character from the Second World War, and very few from the many other conflicts the United Kingdom has been involved in during the last 100 years. The narrative was used to justify the involvement of the United Kingdom and United States troops in the Second Gulf War and the invasion of Iraq in 2003.

Managing the news

Even before the Gulf War started, a special unit in the US military took on the task of news management (Manheim, 1993). In particular, they were interested in the immunisation techniques first suggested by McGuire (1964). The aim of this approach was to prepare the population for some bad news and offer challenges to any likely negative messages.[1] The specific aims of the special unit were to

- keep problems and foul ups in perspective
- preserve the credibility of the army
- prevent surprises
- create the 'right' first impressions and prevent 'false' impressions
- keep everybody calm (Don't Panic!)

An example of this strategy was the way that they dealt with the threat of chemical warfare. The army was aware that Iraq had chemical weapons and it also had evidence of their use in campaigns against the Kurds who were in conflict with the Iraqi government. These weapons were capable of inflicting very heavy casualties on the US forces and rather than ignore the danger or play it down, the special unit initiated a series of briefings with reporters to get the subject on the agenda as early as possible. This strategy prepared people for potentially bad news during the conflict.

Controlling the media

The American government believed that it could only continue the conflict with Iraq while its own public supported the action. They believed that the negative press coverage of the Vietnam War had undermined the will of the American people to continue that war, and they wanted to avoid this happening again. The government needed to control the media's reaction to this conflict but they wanted to avoid excluding the press since this would affect the credibility of the operation. They obtained the result they wanted by flooding the area with journalists.

---

1 A similar technique was used by the British Labour Party up to and during the General Election of 1997 with their 'rapid rebuttals unit'.

The military developed a 'Hometown News Program' which brought local journalists from all over the United States to the Gulf at the army's expense. In news conferences, they all wanted to ask their own questions which were largely repetitive and relatively uninformed. This had the effect of squeezing out the more informed and critical national media. The military was also aware that in the United States the local media have more credibility than the national media who are often seen as cynical. The Hometown News Program brought around 1,500 journalists to the Gulf during the conflict (Manheim, 1993) and helped manage the news output and keep it local and simple. This news management managed to keep damaging items off the public agenda including the idea that American soldiers were being asked to risk their lives for the sake of oil. This could have been very damaging for President Bush because of his connections with Texas oil companies and his personal links with Kuwait made through this oil connection (Wayne, 1993).

Another aspect of the news management by the American military was to avoid all estimates of Iraqi casualties. These were not released until after the conflict when, a government worker followed her normal procedure and released this information to a reporter on request. She was removed from her job and her files disappeared from her desk. The estimates for Iraqi war deaths were 86,194 men, 39,612 women and 32,195 children.

The news for public consumption had one final component and that was the demonisation of the Iraqis. The Kuwaitis employed a consultancy in the United States who spent over $11 million on putting their case across. This agency is reported to have been the source of an infamous story of Iraqi soldiers pulling newborn Kuwaiti children from their incubators so they could steal the equipment. A young woman gave evidence to the American Congress that she had witnessed this first hand. It was later discovered, however, that the young woman was the daughter of the Kuwaiti Ambassador to the United States and she had been coached in her evidence by the consultancy (Manheim, 1993).

3 Civilian campaigns

Personalising the issue

One way of deflecting criticism of a government is to talk about individual people and look at the problems of one person rather than most people. In this way, you can single out a person who has done well and so infer that all people are doing well or could do well. American President Ronald Reagan was often referred to as the Great Communicator and one of his techniques was to personalise issues in this way. For example, when talking on the issue of poverty he referred to a Vietnamese refugee by name and described her rags to riches story since her arrival in the United States. He also talked about a Black woman who had started up a home for the children of drug-addicted mothers. These two stories showed how poverty was a personal issue that could be overcome and that social problems could be dealt with by personal initiative rather than government intervention (Pratkanis & Aronson, 1992). This type of speech can bring about an emotional response in the audience, but it ignores the many counter-examples of people who continue to struggle with poverty and poor conditions.

Look at how often politicians and news outlets personalise issues. Individual cases can be dealt with and provide happy endings to the stories. Structural issues (such as poverty) cannot be solved so easily and don't offer happy endings.

Granfalloon

The minimal group paradigm is a term used to describe the work of Henri Tajfel (for example, 1970) which showed that people can easily be encouraged to support a group of strangers just by drawing attention to some supposed similarity between the individual and the strangers, for example, 'These people are all Capricorns just like you'. The term granfalloon comes from American Science Fiction author Kurt Vonnegut and is used in many texts to describe this effect. Granfalloons are proud and meaningless associations of human beings. The granfalloon has a cognitive and motivational effect. On the cognitive side, it helps to categorise the world and make sense of it. On the motivational side, we derive self-esteem and pride from the groups we belong to, so we are likely to defend our own group and look down on opposing groups.

Politicians use the granfalloon technique to encourage people to feel part of a political or military enterprise and to feel hostile towards people in other groups. An extreme example of this is the use of racial groups as scapegoats. The propaganda used in Nazi Germany identified the Jews as a group of people responsible for the problems of the German people. It was designed to encourage German identity by identifying and demonising people who were not German. It is a technique that was not unique to Nazi Germany, and it is a common technique of politicians to make us feel part of a group of which they are an important part.

Factoids

We like to believe that our attitudes are based on reason and good sense, and that we consider the appropriate evidence before coming to our conclusions about someone or something. This is not always the case, and sometimes we put undue faith in factoids. Factoids are 'facts which have no existence before appearing in a magazine or newspaper' (Norman Mailer cited in Pratkanis & Aronson, 1992, p. 71). An example of this in the area of consumer choice comes from a leaflet circulated in France and referred to as the 'Leaflet of Villejuif' (see Kapferer, 1989). The leaflet, whose source is unknown, was produced in simple type, photocopied and handed around. It said that a number of mass-produced drinks such as Cocoa Cola should be avoided because they contain carcinogens (substances that cause cancer).

The leaflet claimed to come from the Hospital of Villejuif which has a reputation for its cancer work. The hospital, however, denies all knowledge of the leaflet and says the details on the leaflet are incorrect. Despite this, the leaflet has been widely circulated (around half the population report they have read or heard of the leaflet), 19% said they had stopped buying the products mentioned in the leaflet, and many more said they intended to stop buying them. This is an example of how a product can be damaged by a factoid, but the more common example involves advertisers creating factoids to change our behaviour. These factoids often include scientific-looking graphics which show, for example, how a pain-killer works (even though research suggests that we have little understanding of this process), or how shampoo affects your hair.

Fake news

This brings us to the issue of fake news which refers to news stories that contain incorrect information either by accident or design. These stories are often amusing but can be used to undermine people or ideas. The term 'fake news' is new but the attempt to create a belief in falsehoods is certainly not. As long as civilization has recorded and reported ideas, there have been people trying to present themselves in a good light and their opponents in a bad light. You can check out examples of this from ancient Rome and earlier. More recently, in 1924 the Daily Mail (who'd have thought it?) ran a story just before the General Election in which they claimed to have a letter from Moscow Communists to the British Communist Party which suggested that a Labour Government would radicalise the country and initiate a revolution. It is widely believed to have affected the outcome of the election.

So fake news isn't new, but there are increasingly sophisticated attempts to create it in the modern world and to influence societies. Fake news generates money for media companies and this fuels the creation of these stories. In 2016 *The Valley Report* website published an article reporting that a woman was arrested for defecating on her supervisor's desk by way of a resignation letter after she had won a substantial sum from a lottery ticket. We would so like this to be true that we are prepared to believe it. The story was false but despite this, it received 1.7 million reactions and comments on Facebook. Every click exposes you to more promotional messages and adds to the revenue of the social media company. There is no incentive for news outlets to check the quality of news because they can generate more income with bogus but funny items.

Summary

The above two accounts of persuasive messaging in war hopefully give an indication of the style and pervasiveness of psychological operations. The reader can reflect on their own experience of news watching to see how these techniques are still being used. The controversy for psychologists and their involvement with these activities is the same as the controversy addressed in the chapter on war. In what circumstances is it justifiable to use psychological techniques to deceive and coerce people to increase support for military actions and actions that will bring harm to other people? The final section on fake news acts as an introduction to the next section on Big Data.

Big data, psychographics and nudges

Just 25 years ago only about 16 million people used the internet in the whole world (about 0.4% of the people on the planet). Now over 5.2 billion people have internet accounts which is nearly two-thirds of all people on the planet (Internet World Stats, 2021). If we want to influence what people think, feel or do then what better way to do this than to use the internet?

Big data

Our use of the internet and smart cards creates a data trail about our behaviour and much more. Every key press and every swipe of your cards creates a data point, and these data points can be used to profile you and predict your behaviour. Sometimes this can be useful, for example, when your bank notices some unusual behaviour on your cards and blocks it in case it has been stolen.[2] The issue for psychologists and data analysts has been to find techniques to deal with humongous amounts of data and to process the information to give useful results.

The development of analytical techniques has created ways of psychologically profiling individuals without their knowledge using their behaviour online to achieve this. For example, an algorithm was developed that used an individual's 'likes' of public Facebook pages (Kosinski et al., 2013) to automatically predict an individual's personality traits The algorithm mapped onto the most robust model of personality originally developed by McCrae and Costa (1987). Commonly referred to as the Big Five or the OCEAN scale, it has five personality traits which are Openness to experiences, Conscientiousness, Extroversion, Agreeableness, and Neuroticism (see also chapter 4). The algorithm also predicts personal attributes including political and religious views, sexual orientation, ethnicity, intelligence, happiness, use of addictive substances, parental separation, age, and gender. Of course, this doesn't amount to anything unless these profiles are relatively accurate. And, indeed, research does point to their accuracy (Azucar et al., 2018, p. 157).

Not surprisingly, this sort of profiling makes a number of organisations – political, commercial and military – sit up and take notice. If I know what you are thinking and doing and if I have some idea about who you are then I can target information to you to affect your thoughts, feelings and behaviour. Perhaps, I can take the propaganda techniques described above and customise them for individuals.

---

2 Of course this can be quite annoying such as when my card was blocked after I bought Mario Party for my Nintendo Switch because my bank profile suggests I am too old to buy such things.

Psychographics

Psychographics is a methodology that is used to describe the psychological attributes of individuals and groups. Psychographics goes beyond demographic variables such as age and gender and tries to understand the factors that drive behaviour. Research dates back to the 1960s when it focused on consumer rather than political behaviour (Wells, 1975). More recently, however, it has harnessed data and tracking methods to look at the emotional impact of advertising campaigns, and how to tailor persuasive political messages to profiled psychological needs of individuals and groups (Chester & Montgomery, 2017).

One of the (now discredited) players in psychographics was Cambridge Analytica. This company was created in 2013 as one part of the SCL Group which describes itself as a global election management agency. The company has close ties to the UK Conservative Party and the British military.

The CEO of Cambridge Analytica, Alexander Nix asserted that psychographics provides information to political campaigners about what sort of persuasive message needs to be delivered, on what issue, nuanced to what personality types, and to what group of people (Nix, 2016). The company illegally took and used information from Facebook accounts for use with political messaging during elections (Reuters, 2018). In 2016, Cambridge Analytica worked with the Leave Campaign during the Brexit referendum and also with Donald Trump during his successful presidential campaign (Bakir, 2020). The jury is out on the effectiveness of Cambridge Analytica's techniques, but the jury is agreed about the illegality of their methods and the company was shut down. The parent company, however, remains in existence and still provides services to politicians and other organisations.

Psychographics have the potential to give us a lot of insight into behaviour and help promote social planning that is of benefit to the population. Unfortunately, and partly due to the complexity and cost of these analyses, psychographics has been used by the powerful to influence and coerce people into behaviours that benefit these powerful people and organisations.

Nudges

The start of nudge theory is sometimes dated to the publication of Thaler and Sunstein's book *Nudge: Improving Decisions about Health, Wealth and Happiness* in 2008, though some of the ideas had been around before that. It caught the imagination of people with an interest in influencing others and, for example, the British Government set up a nudge unit (known as the Behavioural Insights Team) in 2010. It became a limited company and by 2020, according to its own materials, its work spanned 31 countries in its efforts to 'generate and apply behavioural insights to inform policy, improve public services and deliver results for citizens and society' (The Behavioural Insights Team, 2020). Most recently, the British government has been following a nudge strategy (not altogether successfully) during the global pandemic (The Guardian, 2020).

According to Thaler and Sunstein, a nudge can be defined as 'any aspect of the choice architecture that alters people's behaviour in a predictable way, without forbidding any options or significantly changing their economic incentives. To count as a mere nudge, the intervention must be easy and cheap to avoid' (Thaler & Sunstein, 2008, p. 6). One of the most cited examples of a nudge is the addition of the picture of a fly to urinal basins in the male toilets at Schiphol airport in Amsterdam. This simple nudge gave men something to aim at and reportedly reduced spillage and cleaning costs dramatically.

Another example which is more coercive is the get-out-the-vote button which can be found on Facebook on election day. It was first used in the United States in 2008 and in the United Kingdom for the Scottish Independence Referendum in 2014, and is now used at many elections in many countries (Grassegger, 2018). The button appears in a user's Facebook feed on the day of the election and provides a nudge to vote. It also provides a link to find polling stations, a button to click on that says 'I Voted', and information about how many other Facebook users had clicked this button. Research by Facebook claims that this nudge improves voter turnout (Bond et al., 2012; Jones et al., 2017).

The use of big data to create psychographic profiles and to nudge people towards small behavioural changes has potential for benefits in our society. However, the issue (as described in chapter one) is about control. Who has control over the data and nudges and what are they using it for? It is clear that at present these data are being used by a powerful elite to manipulate the general population, and psychology is complicit with this.

Summary

Propaganda is often presented as a simple process that attempts to change people's behaviour by shouting loudly and using capital letters. Psychology's contribution has been to make this a much more sophisticated process, and a process that is often hard to detect. The messages involve mild distortion of information through to the manufacture of persuasive stories. Propaganda also involves cultural analysis that allows the propagandist to target key issues in people's lives and attempt to change their attitudes and behaviour. With the arrival of Big Data, it is possible to nuance these messages to individuals. Today, when we listen to news messages and promotional messages for products we know that every message has the hand of news management on it. The question is, whose hand is on this bit of news?

References

American Psychological Association (2002). Ethical principles for psychologists and code of conduct. *American Psychologist*, *57*, 1060–1073.

APA (2014). Think again: Men and women share cognitive skills: Research debunks myths about cognitive difference. Available at https://www.apa.org/topics/neuropsychology/men-women-cognitive-skills

APA (2017). How much federal funding is directed to research in psychology? Available at https://www.apa.org/monitor/2017/04/datapoint

APA Ethics Committee (2009). No defense to torture under the APA ethics code. Retrieved September 2010 from http://www.apa.org/news/press/statements/ethics-statement-torture.pdf

Adorno, T.W., Frenkel-Brunswik, G., Levinson, D. J., & Sanford, R.N. (1950). *The Authoritarian Personality*. New York: Harper.

Ashton, M.C., Lee, K., Perugini, M., Szarota, P., de Vries, R.E., Di Blas, L., Boies, K., & De Raad, B. (2004). A six-factor structure of personality-descriptive adjectives: Solutions from psycholexical studies in seven languages. *Journal of Personality and Social Psychology*, *86*(2), 356–366.

Azucar, D., Marengo, D., & Settanni, M. (2018). Predicting the big 5 personality traits from digital footprints on social media: A meta-analysis. *Personality and Individual Differences*, *124*, 150–159. 10.1016/j.paid.2017.12.018

Bakir, V. (2020). Psychological operations in digital political campaigns: Assessing Cambridge analytica's psychographic profiling and targeting. *Frontiers in Communication*, *5*(67). https://www.frontiersin.org/article/10.3389/fcomm.2020.00067. DOI: 10.3389/fcomm.2020.00067

Baldwin, B.T. (1921). In memory of Wilhelm Wundt. By his American students. *The Psychological Review*, *28*(3), 153–188.

Banyard, P. (2007). Book review - Tyranny and the Tyrant. *The Psychologist*, *20*, 494–495.

Bargh, J.A., Chen, M., & Burrows, L. (1996). Automaticity of social behavior: Direct effects of trait construct and stereotype activation on action. *Journal of Personality and Social Psychology*, *71*(2), 230.

Baron, R.A. & Byrne, D. (1991). *Social Psychology: Understanding Human Interactions*. 6th Edition. Boston: Allyn and Bacon.

BBC (2005). US right attacks SpongeBob video. Available at http://news.bbc.co.uk/1/hi/world/americas/4190699.stm.

BBC (2011). Profile, Mohammad Sudique Khan. Available at https://www.bbc.co.uk/news/uk-12621381

BBC (2020). Racism definition: Merriam-Webster to make update after request. Available at https://www.bbc.co.uk/news/world-us-canada-52993306

BBC (2021a). Black scientists say UK research is institutionally racist. Available at https://www.bbc.co.uk/news/science-environment-58795079

BBC (2021b). Cecil Rhodes statue will not be removed by Oxford College. Available at https://www.bbc.co.uk/news/uk-england-oxfordshire-57175057.

Bell, D. (2020). 'I understood when I listened to people's stories'. *The Psychologist*, *33*, P34–P37.

Bell, D. (2021). Resuturing being and knowing. In U. Dutta (Session organizer), *The (Im) Possiblities of a Decolonial Project in Higher Education: Praxis of Entanglements and Radical Hope*. Panel discussion (virtual) held on November 8, 2021.

Bennett, C.M., Baird, A.A., Miller, M.B., & Wolford, G.L. (2010). Neural correlates of interspecies perspective taking in the post-mortem Atlantic Salmon: An argument for proper multiple comparisons correction. *Journal of Serendipitous and Unexpected Results*, *1*(1), 1–5.

Bentall, P. (1992). A proposal to classify happiness as a psychiatric disorder. *Journal of Medical Ethics*, *18*(2), 94–98.

Blackbourne, J. (2011). The evolving definition of terrorism in UK law. *Behavioral Sciences of Terrorism and Political Aggression*, *3*(2), 131–149.

Bloche M.G. & Marks, J.H. (2005). Doctors and interrogators at Guantanamo Bay. *New England Journal of Medicine*, *353*(1), 6–8.

Bol, L. & Strage, A. (1996). The contradiction between teachers' instructional goals and their assessment practices in high school biology courses. *Science Education*, *80*, 145–163.

Bond, R.M., Fariss, C.J., Jones, J.J., Kramer, A.D.I., Marlow, C., Settle, J.E., et al. (2012). A 61-million-person experiment in social influence and political mobilization. *Nature* *489*, 295–298. 10.1038/nature11421

Bordogna, F. (2008). *William James at the Boundaries*. Chicago: University of Chicago Press.

BPS (2013). Classification of behaviour and experience in relation to functional psychiatric diagnoses: Time for a paradigm shift. Available at https://www.bps.org.uk/sites/www.bps.org.uk/files/Member%20Networks/Divisions/DCP/Classification%20of%20behaviour%20and%20experience%20in%20relation%20to%20functional%20psychiatric%20diagnoses.pdf

Bramson, L. & Geothals, G.W. (eds.) (1968). *War: Studies from Psychology, Sociology and Anthropology*, Revised Edition. New York: Basic Books.

British Council (2021). Keeping safe: How to spot and prevent online grooming and re-dicalisation. Available at https://www.britishcouncil.org/anyone-anywhere/explore/dark-side-web/online-grooming-radicalisation

Brooks, V. (2004). Double marking revisited. *British Journal of Educational Studies*, *52* (1), 29–46.

Broverman, I.K., Broverman, D. M., & Clarkson, F.E. (1971). Sex-role stereotypes and clinical judgements of mental health. *Journal of Consulting and Clinical Psychiatry*, *34*, 1–7.

Bryan, D., Kelly, L., & Templer, S. (2011). The failed paradigm of 'terrorism'. *Behavioral Sciences of Terrorism and Political Aggression*, *3*(2), 80–96. 10.1080/19434472.2010.512151

Cahalan, S. (2019). *The Great Pretender*. New York: Grand Central Publishing.

Caplan, P. (1995). *They Say You're Crazy: How the World's Most Powerful Psychiatrists Decide Who's Normal*. New York: Addison-Wesley Publishing Company.

Carraher, T.N., Carraber, D., & Schliemann, A.D. (1985). Mathematics in the streets and in schools. *British Journal of Developmental Psychology*, *3*, 21–29.

Carroll, J.B. (1993). *Human Cognitive Abilities: A Survey of Factor-Analytic Studies*. Cambridge, England: University of Cambridge Press.

Cattell, R.B. (1957). *Personality and Motivation Structure and Measurement*. New York: World Book.

Cattell, R.B. & Butcher, H.J. (1968). *The Prediction of Achievement and Creativity*. Indianapolis: Bobbs-Merrill.

Cattell, R.B., Eber, H.W., & Tatsuoka, M.M. (1970). *The 16-Factor Personality Questionnaire*. Champaign, IL: IPAT.

Ceci, S.J. & Liker, J. (1986). A day at the races: A study of IQ, expertise, and cognitive complexity. *Journal of Experimental Psychology: General, 115*, 255–266.

Césaire, A. (1972). *Discourse on Colonialism*. New York: Monthly Review Press.

Charura, D. & Lago, C. (2021). *Black Identities and White Therapies: Race, Respect and Diversity*. PCCS Books.

Chester, J. & Montgomery, K. (2017). The role of digital marketing in political campaigns. *Internet Policy Reviews, 6*(4). 10.14763/2017.4.773

Clark, K.B. & Clark, M.P. (1939). The development of consciousness of self and the emergence of racial identification in Negro preschool children. *Journal of Social Psychology; Political, Racial and Differential Psychology, 10*(4), 591.

Clark, K.B. & Clark, M.P. (1947). Racial identification and preference among negro children. In E.L. Hartley (Ed.) *Readings in Social Psychology*. New York: Holt, Rinehart, and Winston.

Clark, K.B. & Clark, M.P. (1950). Emotional factors in racial identification and preference in Negro children. *The Journal of Negro Education, 19*(3), 341.

Collins, J. & Hebert, T. (2008). Race and gender images in psychology textbooks. *Race, Gender & Class, 15*(3-4), 300–307.

Connor-Greene, P.A. (2000). Assessing and promoting student learning: Blurring the line between teaching and testing. *Teaching of Psychology, 27*(2), 84–88.

Costa, P.T., Jr. & McCrae, R.R. (1992). *NEO PI–R Professional Manual*. Odessa, FL: Psychological Assessment Resources.

Deaux, K. (1984). From individual difference to social categories: Analysis of a decade's research on gender. *American Psychologist, 39*, 105–116.

Denekens, J.P.M., Nys, H., & Stuer, H. (1999). Sterilisation of incompetent mentally handicapped persons: A model for decision making. *Journal of Medical Ethics, 25*, 237–241.

DiAngelo, R.J. (2018). *White Fragility: Why It's so Hard for White People to Talk About Racism*. London: Penguin.

Donnelly, L. (2013). Students taking 'smart drugs' may be behind soaring Ritalin use. *The Telegraph*. Retrieved from http://www.telegraph.co.uk/health/healthnews/10238660/Students-taking-smart-drugs-may-be-behind-soaring-Ritalin-use.html. (accessed 5 September 2013).

Doyen, S., Klein, O., Pichon, C.-L., & Cleeremans, A. (2012). Behavioral priming: It's all in the mind, but whose mind? *PLoS One, 7*(1), e29081.

Durbin, E.F.M. & Bowlby, J. (1939). *Personal Aggressiveness and War*. New York Chichester, West Sussex: Columbia University Press. 10.7312/durb92284

Durbin, E.F.M. & Bowlby, J. (1938). Personal aggressiveness and war L. Bramson and G.W. Geothals (Eds.) (1968) *War: Studies from Psychology, Sociology and Anthropology*, Revised Edition. (pp. 81–104). New York: Basic Books.

Elmsley, J. (1994). Molecule of the month: Teflon: The non-stick myth that stuck: Did you think that your hi-tech frying pan was a spin-off from the space race? *The Independent*. Retrieved from http://www.independent.co.uk/news/science/molecule-of-the-month-teflon-the-nonstick-myth-that-stuck-did-you-think-that-your-hitech-frying-pan-was-a-spinoff-from-the-space-race-john-emsley-explains-that-the-truth-is-the-other-way-around-1414648.html (accessed 15 May 2015).

Eysenck, H.J. & Eysenck, S.B.G. (1975). *Manual of the Eysenck Personality Questionnaire*. London: Hodder and Stoughton.

Eysenck, H.J. & Eysenck, S.B.G. (1976). *Psychoticism as a Dimension of Personality*. London: Hodder & Stoughton.

Eysenck, H.J. & Eysenck, S.B.G. (1991). *Manual of the Eysenck Personality Scales (EPS Adult): Comprising the EPQ-Revised (EPQ-R), EPQ-R Short Scale, Impulsiveness (IVE) Questionnaire*. London: Hodder & Stoughton.

Eysenck, M.W. (1979). Depth, elaboration, and distinctiveness. In L.S. Cermack & F.I.M. Craik (Eds.) *Levels of Processing in Human Memory* (pp. 89–118). Hillsdale, NJ: Erlbaum.

Fancher, R.E. (1996). *Pioneers of Psychology*, 3rd edition. New York: W.W. Norton.

Fazir-Short, N. (2020). We need to broaden the conversation to institutional bias. *The Psychologist*, *33*, P24–P26. Available at https://thepsychologist.bps.org.uk/volume-33/september-2020/we-need-broaden-conversation-institutional-bias

FBI (2005). Terrorism 2002-05. Available at https://www.fbi.gov/stats-services/publications/terrorism-2002-2005

Ferguson, E. & Cox, T. (1997). The functional dimensions of coping scale: Theory, reliability and validity. *British Journal of Health Psychology*, *2*, 109–129.

Fisher Family Trust (2011). Written evidence submitted by the Fisher Family Trust to the Education Select Committee of the UK Parliament. Available at https://publications.parliament.uk/pa/cm201012/cmselect/cmeduc/851/851vw293.htm

Folkman, S. & Lazarus, R. (1990). Coping and emotion. In A. Monat & R. Lazarus (Eds.) *Stress and Coping*, 3rd edition. New York: Columbia University Press.

Forer, B.R. (1949). The fallacy of personal validation: A classroom demonstration of gullibility. *Journal of Abnormal and Social Psychology*, *44*, 118–123.

Frances, A. (2013). One manual shouldn't dictate US mental health research. *New Scientist*. Available at https://www.newscientist.com/article/dn23490-one-manual-shouldnt-dictate-us-mental-health-research/#ixzz7COMBRQch

Freud, S. (1964). [1933]. Why War? In. *The Standard Edition of the Complete Works of Sigmund Freud*, vol. XXII, London: Hogarth Press. pp. 197–218.

Furnham, A. & Varian, C. (1988). Predicting and accepting personality test scores. *Personality and Individual Differences*, *9*, 735–748.

Galatzer-Levy, I. & Bryant, R. (2013). 636,120 ways to have posttraumatic stress disorder. *Perspectives on Psychological Science*, *8*(6), 651–662.

Gale, A. (1990). Applying psychology to the psychology degree: Pass with first class honours, or miserable failure? *The Psychologist*, *11*, 483–488.

Gill, J.K. (2020). The discomfort of institutional racism. *The Psychologist*, *33*, P2. Available at https://thepsychologist.bps.org.uk/volume-33/december-2020/discomfort-institutional-racism

Gilovich, T. (1981). Seeing the past in the present: The effects of associations to familiar events on judgements and decisions. *Journal of Personality and Social Psychology*, *40*, 797–808.

Gladwin, T. (1970). *East is a Big Bird: Navigation and logic on Puluwat atoll*. Cambridge, MA: Harvard University Press.

Gómez-Ordóñez, L., Adams, G., Ratele, K., Suffla, S., Stevens, G., & Reddy, G. (2021). Decolonising psychological science: Encounters and cartographies of resistance. *The Psychologist, 34*, 54–57.

Goodey, C.F. (2011). *A History of Intelligence and 'Intellectual Disability': The Shaping of Psychology in Early Modern Europe.* Farnham: Ashgate.

Gould, S.J. (1978). Women's Brains. *New Scientist*, 364–366.

Gould, S.J. (1981). *The Mismeasure of Man.* Harmondsworth: Penguin.

Gould, S.J. (1982). A nation of morons. *New Scientist* (6 May 1982), 349–352.

Gould, S.J. (1996). *The Mismeasure of Man*, 2nd edition. London: Norton.

GOV.UK (2021). Detentions under the Mental Health Act. Available at https://www.ethnicity-facts-figures.service.gov.uk/health/mental-health/detentions-under-the-mental-health-act/latest

GOV.UK (2021). Prevent duty guidance: For higher education institutions in England and Wales. Available at https://www.gov.uk/government/publications/prevent-duty-guidance/prevent-duty-guidance-for-higher-education-institutions-in-england-and-wales

Grassegger, H. (2018). "Facebook says its 'voter button' is good for turnout. But should the tech giant be nudging us at all?" *The Guardian.* Available at https://www.theguardian.com/technology/2018/apr/15/facebook-says-it-voter-button-is-good-for-turn-but-should-the-tech-giant-be-nudging-us-at-all

Gray, J.A. & McNaughton, N. (2000). *The Neuropsychology of Anxiety: An Enquiry into the Functions of the Septo-hippocampal System,* 2nd edition. Oxford: Oxford University Press.

Greely, H., Sahakian, B., Harris, J., Kessler, R. C., Gazzaniga, M., Campbell, P., & Farah, M. J. (2008). Towards responsible use of cognitive-enhancing drugs by the healthy. *Nature, 456,* 702–705. 10.1038/456702a

Gregory, W. & Burroughs, W. (1989). *Applied Psychology.* Glenview, Illinois: Scott Foresman.

Grossman, D. (1995). *On Killing.* London: Back Bay Books.

Guthrie, R.V. (1998). *Even the Rat Was White: A Historical View of Psychology,* 2nd edition. Boston: Allyn and Bacon.

Hall, I. & Higgs, S. (2005). Primary school students' perceptions of interactive whiteboards. *Journal of Computer Assisted Learning, 21*(2), 102–117.

Halonen, J.S., Bosack, T., Clay, S., McCarthy, M., Dunn, D.S., Hill, G.W., et al. (2003). A rubric for learning, teaching and assessing scientific inquiry in psychology. *Teaching of Psychology, 30*(3), 196–208.

Haney, C., Banks, C., & Zimbardo, P. (1973). A study of prisoners and guards in a simulated prison. *Naval Research Review, 30,* 4–17.

Haslam, A. & Reicher, S. (2003). A tale of two prison experiments: Beyond a role-based explanation of tyranny. *Psychology Review, 9*(4), 2–6.

Haslam, S.A. & Reicher, S.D. (2017). 50 Years of "Obedience to Authority": From blind conformity to engaged followership. *Annual Review of Law and Social Science, 13,* 59–78.

Hergenhahn, B.R. (2001). *An Introduction to the History of Psychology*, 4th edition. Belmont: Wadsworth.

Herrnstein, R.J. (1971). I.Q., *The Atlantic Monthly, 228,* 43–64.

Herrnstein, R.J. & Murray, C. (1994). *The Bell Curve.* New York: The Free Press.

Hewstone, M., Stroebe, W., Codol, J.P., & Stephenson, G. (1988). *Introduction to Social Psychology: A European Perspective.* Oxford: Blackwell.

Hovland, C.I., Janis, I.L., & Kelly, H.H. (1953). *Communication and Persuasion.* New Haven, CT: Yale University Press.

Hovland, C.I., Lumsdaine, A.A., & Sheffield, F.D. (1949). Studies in social psychology in World War II. *Vol. 3: Experiments in Mass Communication.* Princeton, NJ: Princeton University Press.

Hudson, R. (1999). Sociology and psychology of terrorism: Who becomes a terrorist and why? US Library of Congress. Available at https://www.loc.gov/rr/frd/pdf-files/Soc_Psych_of_Terrorism.pdf

Internet World Stats (2021). *Internet Growth Statistics,* Available at tinyurl.com/6aaxc2

IRR (Institute of Race Relations) (2021). Health and mental health statistics. Available at https://irr.org.uk/research/statistics/health/

James-Myers, L. (1988). Understanding an Afrocentric world view. *Introduction to an Optimal Psychology.*Dubuque, Iowa: Kendall/Hunt Pub. Co.

James, H., Jr. (1920). *The letters of William James.* Boston: Atlantic Monthly Press.

James, W. (1910). The moral equivalent of war. In L. Bramson and G.W. Geothals (Eds.) *(1968) War: Studies from Psychology, Sociology and Anthropology, Revised Edition* (pp. 21–31). New York: Basic Books.

Jäncke, L. (2018). Sex/gender differences in cognition, neurophysiology, and neuroanatomy. *F1000Research,* 7, F1000 Faculty Rev-805. 10.12688/f1000research.13917.1

Jankowski, G.S. (2021). Students' understanding and support for anti-racism in universities. *British Journal of Social Psychology.* 10.1111/BJSO.12482

Jankowski, G., Gillborn, S., & Sandle, R. (2017). Advancing BME Psychology. *The Psychologist, 30*(10), p2.

Johnstone, L. (2014). *A Straight Talking Introduction to Psychiatric Diagnosis.* Lucy Johnstone, PCCS Books.

Johnstone, L. (2018). Psychological formulation as an alternative to psychiatric diagnosis. *Journal of Humanistic Psychology, 58*(1), 30–46.

Jones, E.S. (1938). Reliability in marking examinations. *The Journal of Higher Education, 9*(8), 436–439.

Jones, J.J., Bond, R.M., Bakshy, E., Eckles, D., & Fowler, J.H. (2017). Social influence and political mobilization: Further evidence from a randomized experiment in the 2012 U.S. presidential election. *PLoS One, 12,* 4. 10.1371/journal.pone.0173851

Kamin, L. (1977). *The Science and Politics of IQ.* Harmondsworth: Penguin.

Kapferer, J.N. (1989). A mass poisoning rumour in Europe. *Public Opinion Quarterly, 53,* 467–481.

Kaplan, R.M. & Saccuzzo, D.P. (1993). *Psychological Testing: Principles Applications and Issues.* Pacific Grove, California: Brooks/Cole.

Keys, A., Brozeck, J., Henschel, A., Mickelson, O., & Taylor, H.L. (1950). *The Biology of Human Starvation,* Minn-Press.

Kline, P. (1991). *Intelligence: The Psychometric View.* London: Routledge.

Kline, P. (1993). *The Handbook of Psychological Testing.* London: Routledge.

Kosinski, M., Stillwell, D., & Graepel, T. (2013). Private traits and attributes are predictable from digital records of human behavior. *Proceedings of National Academy of Science USA, 110,* 5802–5805. 10.1073/pnas.1218772110

Kutchins, H. & Kirk, S. (1999). *Making Us Crazy: DSM - The Psychiatric Bible and the Creation of Mental Disorders.* London: Constable.

Levant, R. (2007). Visit to the U.S. Joint Task Force Station at Guantanamo Bay: A first-person account. *Military Psychology, 19*(1), 1–7.

Lifton, R.J. (2004). *Thought Reform and the Psychology of Totalism: A Study of 'Brainwashing' in China.* London: Victor Gollanz.

Littlewood, R. & Lipsedge, M. (1997). *Aliens and Alienists,* 3rd edition, Unwin Hyman.

Longden, E. (2013). The voices in my head. *TED.* Available at https://www.ted.com/talks/eleanor_longden_the_voices_in_my_head

Lord, A.B. (1960). *The Singer of Tales.* Cambridge, MA: Harvard University Press.

Lutus, P. (2020). *Psychology and Neuroscience.* Available at https://www.arachnoid.com/psychology_and_neuroscience/index.html

Maccoby, E.E. & Jacklin, C. (1974). *The Psychology of Sex Differences.* Stanford, Calif: Stanford University Press.

Manheim, J.B. (1993). The War of Images: Strategic Communication in the Gulf Conflict. In S. Renshon (Ed.) *The Political Psychology of the Gulf War* (pp. 179–155). Pittsburg: Pittsburg University Press.

Mark, L.S., Warm, J.S., & Huston, R.L. (1987). *Ergonomics and Human Factors: Recent Research.* New York: Springer-Verlag.

Marsden, P. & Attia, S. (2005). A deadly contagion? *The Psychologist, 18*(3), 152–155.

Marshall, S.L.A. (1978). *Men Against Fire.* Gloucester, MA: Peter Smith.

Masicampo, E.J. & Lalande, D.R. (2012). A peculiar prevalence of *p* values just below .05. *Quarterly journal of Experimental Psychology,* PMID: 22853650.

Maslow, A. (1958). A philosophy of psychology. *Main Currents, 13,* 27–32.

Matthews, G., Deary, I.J., & Whiteman, M.C. (2003). *Personality Traits.* Cambridge: Cambridge University Press.

McCrae, R.R. & Costa, P.T., Jr. (1985). Updating Norman's "adequate taxonomy": Intelligence and personality dimensions in natural language and in questionnaires. *Journal of Personality and Social Psychology, 49,* 710–721.

McCrae, R.R. & Costa, P.T. (1987). Validation of the five-factor model of personality across instruments and observers. *Journal of Personality and Social Psychology, 52,* 81–90. 10.1037/0022-3514.52.1.81

McCrae, R.R. & Costa, P.T. (1997). Personality trait structure as a human universal. *American Psychologist, 52*(5), 509–516.

McDougall, W. (1915). *An Introduction to Social Psychology.* London: Methuen.

McGuire, W.J. (1964). Inducing resistance to persuasion: Some contemporary approaches. In L. Berkowitz (Ed.) *Advances in Experimental Social Psychology, 1.* New York: Academic.

McGuire, W.J. (1973). Persuasion, resistance and attitude change. In I. Pool, et al. (Eds.) *Handbook of Communication* (pp. 216–252). Skokie, IL, USA: Rand McNally.

McGuire, W.J. (1985). Attitudes and attitude change. In G. Lindzey and E. Aronson (Eds.) *Handbook of Social Psychology.* New York: Random House.

Mead, M. (1940). Warfare is only an invention - Not a biological necessity. In L. Bramson and G.W. Geothals (Eds.) *(1968) War: Studies from Psychology, Sociology and Anthropology,* Revised edition (pp. 269–274). New York: Basic Books.

Medoff, D. (2009). Freud's reply to Einstein on delivering mankind from war. *Peace Review, 21*(4), 437–441. 10.1080/10402650903323413.

Meltzoff, A.N. & Moore, M.K. (1977). Imitation of facial and manual gestures by human neonates. *Science, 198,* 74–78.

Meltzoff, A.N. & Moore, M.K. (1983). Newborn infants imitate adult facial gestures. *Child Development, 54,* 702–709.

Memmi, A. (1999). *Racism.* University of Minnesota Press.

Memon, A., Taylor, K., Mohebati, L.M., et al. (2016). Perceived barriers to accessing mental health services among black and minority ethnic (BME) communities: A qualitative study in Southeast England. *BMJ Open, 6,* e012337.

Milgram, S. (1974). *Obedience to Authority: An Experimental View*. London: Tavistock.

Miller, G. (1969). Psychology as a means of promoting human welfare. *American Psychologist*, *24*, 1063–1075.

Nature Communications (2014). Publishers withdraw more than 120 Gibberish Science and Engineering Papers. Available at https://www.scientificamerican.com/article/publishers-withdraw-more-than-120-gibberish-science-and-engineering-papers/

Neisser, U., Boodoo, G., Bouchard, T.J., Jr., Boykin, A.W., Brody, N., Ceci, S.J., Halpern, D.F., Loehlin, J.C., Perloff, R., Sternberg, R.J., & Urbina, S. (1996). Intelligence: Knowns and unknowns. *American Psychologist*, *51*(2), 77–101. https://doi.org/10.1037/0003-066X.51.2.77.

Newstead, S.E. & Dennis, I. (1994). Examiners examined: The reliability of exam marking in psychology. *The Psychologist*, 7, 216–219.

Nix, A. (2016). The power of big data and psychographics in the electoral process, In *The Concordia Annual Summit (New York, NY)*. Available at https://www.youtube.com/watch?v=n8Dd5aVXLCc (accessed 26 March 2020).

Nobles, W.W. (1976). Extended self. Rethinking the so-called Negro self-concept. *Journal of Black Psychology*, *2*, 15–24.

O'Connell, A.N. and Russo, N.F. (Eds.) (2001). *Models of Achievement: Reflections of Eminent Women in Psychology*. New York: Columbia University Press.

Office for National Statistics (2021). *Updating Ethnic Contrasts in Deaths Involving the Coronavirus (COVID-19)*, England: 24 January 2020 to 31 March 2021. Available at https://www.ons.gov.uk/peoplepopulationandcommunity/birthsdeathsandmarriages/deaths/articles/updatingethniccontrastsindeathsinvolvingthecoronaviruscovid19englandandwales/24january2020to31march2021

OfS (2021). Office for Students. Available at https://www.officeforstudents.org.uk/

Oostenbroek, J., Suddendorf, T., Nielsen, M., Redshaw, J., Kennedy-Costantini, S., Davis, J., Clark, S., & Slaughter, V. (2016). Comprehensive longitudinal study challenges the existence of neonatal imitation in humans. *Current Biology*, *26*(10), 1334–1338.

Open Science Collaboration (2015). Estimating the reproducibility of psychological science. *Science*, *349*, 6251. 10.1126/science.aac4716

Park, D.C. & Radford, J.P. (1998). Reconstructing a history of involuntary sterilisation. *Disability and Society*, *13*, 317–342.

Paulhus, D.L. & Williams, K.M. (2002). The dark triad of personality: Narcissism, Machiavellianism, and psychopathy. *Journal of Research in Personality*, *36*(6), 556–563.

Philogene, G. (Ed.) (2004). *Racial Identity in Context: The Legacy of Kenneth B. Clark*. Washington: APA.

Pilger, J. (1975). *The Last Day London*. Mirror Group Books.

Pilger, J. (1989). *Heroes*. London: Pan.

Pope, K. & Gutheil, T. (2009). The interrogation of detainees: How doctors' and psychologists' ethical policies differ. *British Medical Journal*, *338*, 1178– 1180.

Pratkanis, A.R. & Aronson, E. (1992). *Age of Propaganda: The Everyday Use and Abuse of Persuasion*. New York: W.H. Freeman.

Pratkanis. A.R., Greenwald, A.G., Leippe, M.R., & Baumgardner, M.H. (1988). In search of reliable persuasion effects. III. The sleeper effect is dead. Long live the sleeper effect. *Journal of Personality and Social Psychology*, *54*. 203–218.

Rauscher, F.H., Shaw, G.L., & Ky, K.N. (1993). Music and spatial task performance. *Nature*, *365*, 611.

Reicher, S. & Haslam, S.A. (2006). Rethinking the psychology of tyranny: The BBC prison study. *British Journal of Social Psychology*, *45*, 1–40.

Reicher, S. & Haslam, A. (2009). FORUM: The real world. *The Psychologist, 22*(6), 469.

Renshon, S.A. (Ed.) (1993). *The Political Psychology of the Gulf War*. Pittsburg: Pittsburg University Press.

Reuters (2018). "Factbox: Who is Cambridge Analytica and What Did It Do?". *U.S.* Available at https://www.reuters.com/article/us-facebook-cambridge-analytica-factbox/factbox-who-is-cambridge-analytica-and-what-did-it-do-idUSKBN1GW07F

Richards, G. (2002). *Putting Psychology in its Place: A Critical Historical Overview*. London: Routledge.

Richards, G. (2012). *'Race', Racism and Psychology*. London: Psychology Press.

Ritzer, G. (1993). *The McDonaldization of Society*. Thousand Oaks, CA: Pine Forge.

Robinson, J. (2021). Antidepressant prescribing up 6% in last three months of 2020. *The Pharmaceutical Journal*. Available at https://pharmaceutical-journal.com/article/news/antidepressant-prescribing-up-6-since-2019.

Romme, M., Escher, S., Dillon, J., & Corstens, D. (2009). *Living with Voices: 50 Stories of Recovery*. PCCS Books.

Ronson, J. (2005). *The Men Who Stare at Goats*. London: Simon & Schuster. Rose, S.C.

Ronson, J. (2011). *The Psychopath Test*. London: Picador.

Rose, S., Kamin, L.J., & Lewontin, R.C. (1984). *Not in Our Genes: Biology, Ideology and Human Nature*. Harmondsworth: Penguin.

Rose, S.C., Bisson, J., Churchill, R., & Wessely, S. (2002). Psychological debriefing for preventing posttraumatic stress disorder (PTSD). *Cochrane Database of Systematic Reviews*, Issue 2. Art. No.: CD000560. 10.1002/14651858.CD000560

Rubin, G.J., Brewin, C.R., Greenberg, N., Simpson, J., & Wessely, S. (2005). Psychological and behavioural reactions to the bombings in London on 7 July 2005: Cross sectional survey of a representative sample of Londoners. *BMJ (Clinical Research Ed.), 331*(7517), 606. 10.1136/bmj.38583.728484.3A

Rushton, J. (1990). Race differences, r/K theory and a reply to Flynn. *The Psychologist, 5*, 195–198.

Sahakian, B., & Morein-Zamir. (2007, December 20). Professor's little helper. *Nature, 450*, 1157–1159. doi:10.1038/4501157a

Scholarlyoa (2019). https://scholarlyoa.com/bogus-journal-accepts-profanity-laced-anti-spam-paper/

Schröder, A., Vulink, N., & Denys, D. (2013). Misophonia: Diagnostic criteria for a new psychiatric disorder. *PLoS One, 8*(1), e54706. 10.1371/journal.pone.0054706

Schultz, D.P. (1996). *A History of Modern Psychology*, 6th edition. Orlando, USA: Harcourt Brace.

Shallice, T. (1973). The Ulster depth interrogation techniques and their relation to sensory deprivation research. *Cognition, 1*(4), 385–405.

Sherif, M. (1956). Experiments in group conflict. *Scientific American, 195*, 54–58.

Shevlin, M. & Miles, J. (1998). Cronbach's alpha: Not always a lower-bound estimate of reliability. Northern Ireland Branch of the British Psychological Society, Carrigart, C. Donegal.

Shevlin, M.E. (1995). An exploratory and theoretical examination of measurement: Reliability, assessment and control. *Ph.D. thesis, University of Ulster*.

Shields, S. (1978). Sex and the biased scientist. *New Scientist, 7/12/78*, 752–754.

Shils, E.A. & Janowitz, M. (1948). The impact of propaganda on Wehrmacht solidarity. In H. Brown & R. Stevens (Eds.) *(1975) Social Behaviour and Experience: Multiple Perspectives.* London: Hodder and Stoughton.

Shotter, J. (1975). *Images of Man in Psychological Research London*: Methuen.

Sigel, R.S. (1964). Effect of partisanship on the perception of political candidates. *Public Opinion Quarterly, 28,* 488–496.

Silke, A. (2004). Terrorism, 9/11 and psychology. *The Psychologist, 17*(9), 518–521.

Skinner, B.F. (1960). Pigeons in a Pelican. *American Psychologist, 15,* 28–37.

Skinner, B.F. (1972). *Beyond Freedom and Dignity.* Harmondsworth: Penguin.

Sky News (2021). Sickle cell disease: MPs call for major changes after inquiry report reveals shocking failures and racist attitudes in care of patients. Available at https://news.sky.com/story/sickle-cell-disease-mps-call-for-major-changes-after-inquiry-report-reveals-shocking-failures-and-racist-attitudes-in-care-of-patients-12469015

Smith, P.B. & Bond, M.H. (1993). *Social Psychology Across Cultures: Analysis and Perspectives.* London: Harvester Wheatsheaf.

Soldz, S. (2007). A profession struggles to save its soul: Psychologists, *Guantanamo and torture. Psychoanalytic Activist.* Washington, DC: American Psychological Association.

Spann, W. (1975). Rechtsgrundlagen der operativen Sterilisation beim Mann und beider Frau in der Bundesrepublik Deutschland. *Geburtshilfe Frauenheilkunde, 35,* 501–503.

Stapel, D. & Lindenberg, S. (2011). Coping with chaos: How disordered contexts promote stereotyping and discrimination. *Science, 332*(6026), 251–253. Available at https://www.science.org/doi/abs/10.1126/science.1201068

Steele, K.M., Bass, K.E., & Crook, M.D. (1999). The mystery of the Mozart effect - Failure to replicate. *Psychological Science, 10,* 366–369.

Stein, M., Walker, J., & Forde, D. (1996). Public-speaking fears in a community sample: Prevalence, impact on functioning, and diagnostic classification. *Archives of General Psychiatry, 53,* 169–174.

Strack, F., Martin, L.L., & Stepper, S. (1988). Inhibiting and facilitating conditions of facial expressions: A non-obtrusive test of the facial feedback hypothesis. *Journal of Personality and Social Psychology, 54,* 768–777.

Stubblefield, A. (2007). '"Beyond the pale': Tainted whiteness, cognitive disability, and eugenic sterilization". *Hypatia: A Journal of Feminist Philosophy, 22*(2), 162–181. 10.1111/j.1527-2001.2007.tb00987.x

Summerfield, D. (2000). War and mental health: A brief overview. *British Medical Journal, 321,* 232–235.

Swank, R. (1949). Combat exhaustion. *Journal of Nervous and Mental Disorders, 9,* 369–376.

Szasz, T.S. (1960). The myth of mental illness. *American Psychologist, 15,* 113–118.

Tajfel, H. (1970). Experiments in intergroup discrimination. *Scientific American, 223,* 96–102.

Taylor, A.J.P. (1963). *The First World War: An Illustrated History.* Harmondsworth: Penguin.

Thaler, R., & Sunstein, C. (2008). *Nudge: Improving Decisions About Health, Wealth and Happiness.* London: Penguin.

The Behavioural Insights Team (2020). Available at https://www.bi.team/about-us/

The Guardian (2004). Israel assassinates Hamas leader. Available at https://www.theguardian.com/world/2004/mar/22/israel1

The Guardian (2019). Churchill's policies contributed to 1943 Bengal famine – study. Available at https://www.theguardian.com/world/2019/mar/29/winston-churchill-policies-contributed-to-1943-bengal-famine-study

The Guardian (2020). Why is the government relying on nudge theory to fight coronavirus? Available at https://www.theguardian.com/commentisfree/2020/mar/13/why-is-the-government-relying-on-nudge-theory-to-tackle-coronavirus

Thompson, J. (1985). *Psychological Aspects of Nuclear War*. Leicester: BPS.

Wagenmakers, E.-J., Beek, T., Dijkhoff, L., Gronau, Q.F., Acosta, A., Adams, R.B., Jr., Albohn, D.N., et al. (2016). Registered Replication Report: Strack, Martin, & Stepper (1988). *Perspectives on Psychological Science*, *11*(6), 917–928.

Wakeling, P. (2010). International Benchmarking Review of Psychology Briefing document: Statistical overview and commentary. *BPS*. Available at https://esrc.ukri.org/files/research/research-and-impact-evaluation/uk-psychology-statistical-overview/

Watson J.B. (1930). *Behaviorism* (Revised Edition). New York: Harpers.

Watson, J.B. (1913). Psychology as the behaviorist views it. *Psychological Review*, *20*, 158–178.

Watson, P. (1980). *War on the Mind: The Military Uses and Abuses of Psychology*. London: Penguin.

Waugh, M.J. (1997). Keeping the home fires burning. *The Psychologist*, *10*, 361–363.

Wayne, S.J. (1993). President Bush goes to war: A psychological interpretation from a distance. In S. Renshon (Ed.) *The Political Psychology of the Gulf War*(pp. 29–47). Pittsburg: Pittsburg University Press.

Weiss, D.S. & Marmar, C.R. (1996). The impact of event scale – Revised. In J. Wilson & T. M. Keane (Eds.) *Assessing Psychological Trauma and PTSD* (pp. 399–411). New York: Guilford.

Wells, W.D. (1975). Psychographics: A critical review. *Journal of Marketing Research*, *12*, 196–213. doi: 10.1177/002224377501200210

Wessely, S. (2006). What's the worst idea on the mind? *The Psychologist*, *19*(9), 518–519. Available at https://thepsychologist.bps.org.uk/volume-19/edition-9/news

Williams, J.H. (1987). *Psychology of Women*, 3rd edition. New York: Norton.

Windle, C. & Vallance, T.R. (1964). The future of military psychology: Paramilitary psychology. *American Psychologist*, *19*(2), 119.

Wood, E. & Attfield, J. (2003). *Play, Learning and the Early Childhood Curriculum*, 2nd edition. London: Sage.

Zimbardo, P. (2007). *The Lucifer Effect – Understanding How Good People Turn Evil*. London: Ebury.

Index

For Product Safety Concerns and Information please contact our EU
representative GPSR@taylorandfrancis.com
Taylor & Francis Verlag GmbH, Kaufingerstraße 24, 80331 München, Germany